The
Emotional
Intelligence
of Jesus

The Emotional Intelligence of Jesus

Relational Smarts for Religious Leaders

ROY M. OSWALD and
ARLAND JACOBSON

An Alban Institute Book

ROWMAN & LITTLEFIELD
Lanham • Boulder • New York • London

Published by Rowman & Littlefield
A wholly owned subsidary of The Rowman & Littlefield Publishing Group, Inc.
4501 Forbes Boulevard, Suite 200, Lanham, Maryland 20706
www.rowman.com

Unit A, Whitacre Mews, 26-34 Stannary Street, London SE11 4AB

British Library Cataloguing in Publication Information Available

Library of Congress Cataloging-in-Publication Data
Oswald, Roy M.
  The emotional intelligence of Jesus : relational smarts for religious leaders / Roy
M. Oswald and Arland Jacobson.
      pages cm
  "An Alban Institute book."
  ISBN 978-1-56699-779-9 (cloth : alk. paper) — ISBN 978-1-56699-780-5
(pbk. : alk. paper) — ISBN 978-1-56699-781-2 (electronic) 1. Christianity—
Psychology. 2. Emotional intelligence. 3. Jesus Christ. 4. Interpersonal
relations—Religious aspects—Christianity. I. Title.
  BR110.O77 2015
  253'.2—dc23   2014036006

Contents

Foreword

The Emotional Intelligence of Jesus

WHO *is* Jesus, and how do we account for his extraordinary power to shape the lives of individuals and of society?

The question has haunted all of us—those who call themselves Christians as well as almost anyone who tries to understand the energies that shape our world.

We ponder and reflect on it, and many of us pray about it, but somehow we never seem fully to solve the riddle. He remains a figure of intriguing mystery as well of deep piety and, for me and many others, a figure who energizes, attracts, and empowers.

Almost every generation produces great minds who struggle to grasp the dilemma of his powerlessness at his end, as well as the continuing power of his influence.

From the time of the Enlightenment, many of those struggling to understand Jesus have used new tools of historical and literary criticism to unpack the written record left by Jesus' associates—in the gospels and epistles, as well as the historical records of the age. The books about him have had no end. And every book has had its devotees and its critics.

Theories abounded and multiplied, each with critics and supporters, perhaps culminating in efforts like those of Albert Schwietzer's monumental *The Quest of the Historical Jesus*.

Late in the nineteenth century, as the world and societies changed, the tools of understanding also changed. Even as some of the traditional methods of study—historical and literary criticism—matured and deepened, brand-new methods joined the fray.

Psychology burst on the scene with thinkers like William James and Sigmund Freud. They and their associates were attracted to the deep questions about how this person and religion itself had the impact that they had on millions of ordinary people.

Throughout the twentieth century, these questions, which seemed to reach the deepest, caused the most perplexity and generated the most antagonism as well as the most hope. Successive generations have produced other waves of thought attempting to understand this man and his impact.

At the same time, the practical work of leading communities spun off in dozens of traditions (denominations, churches, etc.) and brought about the emergence of teachers, managers, and executives tasked to lead and teach the generations who were called to follow this strange Jew who had died tragically in Palestine. It was those teachers and leaders who struggled the hardest to work on these questions, to "make sense" of this mysterious man.

In my own time, my training as pastor in the Anglican tradition was heavily influenced by educational processes indebted to psychological learning and filtered through a process we called clinical pastoral education (CPE). By that time, the groups seeking clarity about Jesus in religious worlds were also impacted by the fringe disciplines of management science and social science, as well as the messy deposit of arguments left over from the various processes of the nineteenth century.

The simple questions about Jesus had morphed into newer questions—because our world had newer questions to ask—about what "a leader" was, and even what "community" was (since all churches were also communities of some sort).

New waves assaulted our understanding—Bion, Winnicott, and Reed gave newer interpretations of the psychological world. We wondered about the category of "attachment theory" and what it had to do with everything. Wittgenstein and Polanyi provided differing slants on what we could understand about "meaning" and "words." We found that our world was enduring a civil war between the idea of "information" and the idea of "wisdom," and technology confused us about it all. And, to tell the truth, technology inundated us with floods of material we rarely could digest.

Burgeoning on top of this wealth of new knowledge, our extraordinary community of science woke up to the realization that we, who wanted so badly to understand, were partly confused because we had no clear sense of how we think or how we understand. Voilà! *Brain science*! Across the world scientists turned their attention to trying to figure out what "mind" was and what the "brain" really did.

Whole new arenas, whole new ways of thinking, whole new disciplines of study began, and are still beginning, to emerge.

Many nineteenth- and early twentieth-century efforts to understand the psychology of individuals and the dynamics of groups filtered into the leadership of local religious communities through clinical pastoral education. CPE-educated pastors, executives, and pastoral theology professors brought ideas into the groups and people who made up religious congregations across the country. Of course, *some* groups found themselves allergic to these ways of thinking and opted out of this form of knowledge—leading to an unfortunate gap in the ability of some religious groups to use potentially helpful resources.

I came to call groups like CPE "linking organizations"—a useful, but not widely used, strategy for spreading useful information. The "linking" locates the organization as one with two foci—one on an important area in which specialists are doing in-depth research, and the other on grassroots groups and individuals who need to know what the researchers have found. (The concept comes from work done in the federal government, where they decided to develop the role of the "research utilization specialist" as one who takes the basic research knowledge and "translates" it into hands-on activity that ordinary people can grasp and do. In my own experience, the best example of this is the county agents across the country whose task is to know what is happening in agricultural research in universities, and to take what fits their county and turns it into stuff their farmers can work with. Not many farmers, in my day, were able to keep up with what the pests or pesticides the universities were testing—but the county agent was somebody they knew and who knew them. He *knew* which farmer needed what and what language he needed to use to teach him. [Personal plea: With all the new knowledge abounding today, why don't the churches get, or hire, or recruit, or just convince some of our brilliant lay scientists to *be* a research utilization specialist for their pastor or executive? I mean, what does a college chaplain actually *do* these days?])

My point here: Roy Oswald and Arland Jacobson are, in this book, operating as research utilization specialists for us in the churches and religious institutions.

Let me simplify (perhaps even oversimplify) what that means—because that is why I wanted to write a foreword for this book even before I saw the manuscript.

There are hundreds of specialist researchers working around the world in private and university laboratories trying to figure out how our brains work. The history of this work is fairly new, and its scope is fast increasing. I'll never read much of it, except maybe an article or two in a magazine. Also, there are thousands of professionals, and hundreds more researchers and professors and, yes, consultants, trying to understand how many people can work together on common concerns—in short, how management happens and what it takes to do it. There will be more magazine articles about that, and more of us *will* probably read some of the new information they have. Indeed, in the field of management, we are likely to read important stuff in the business sections of our newspaper (if we still take a newspaper).

My thesis here, and the thesis underpinning this whole book, is that people in congregations, and especially the leaders of those congregations, need to know some (though not all) of what those brain scientists and management researchers are learning. They may very urgently need to know where those two specialist groups are working on things that fit together and that potentially might really improve what we do and how we manage the local congregations for which we are responsible.

This book is not going to tell you all that these people are doing. Heaven forbid! It is not going to tell you *all* there is to know about new brain science and congregational management. But Oswald and Jacobson have discovered one very promising arena (and I concur with them) in which management science and brain studies have opened up some helpful directions.

The key connector for this is Daniel Goleman. You will learn a lot more about him in this book. His entry point is his work in human organizations. In that work, he has collaborated with and learned from a lot of brain science I don't have time to read.

His primary insights are in his book, *Emotional Intelligence*, which connects the best of management understanding and introduces you to relevant brain science. But let me be clear—this is cutting-edge learning we are talking about. We do not want *anybody* to take this as the last word, although it *is* the best we know for right now. We are sure somebody is now working on stuff that will go beyond where we are—you may well be one who does. This book is not about the final truth; instead, it is an invitation to you to join us in doing and searching—indeed, that is part of emotional intelligence.

But the link between Goleman and the brain scientists is not the critical linkage. The critical linkage is the one provided by Oswald and Jacobson. They *are* researchers and teachers, but that is not where their hearts lie. Their hearts are the hearts of pastors. They love (and are frustrated by) the church. They see as their brothers and sisters those who lead congregations. They see those loaded down with the responsibilities of "bishop" or "executive," and they love to support them, whether it is in crying together over a disaster or celebrating one of the great ones. They respect and love the ones who sit next to them in the pews of their local parish on Sundays.

It is Oswald and Jacobson who bring us the other side of the linkage as we try to be a "linking organization." In this book they bring all the research of people like Goleman and the brain scientists, but they hold those extraordinary discoveries up against Jesus and his example of leadership. This book looks to Jesus for what he is and means in leadership— Jesus who teaches us leadership, who is our exemplar of leadership, and who empowers us in our leadership.

Loren B. Mead
Falls Church, VA

Prologue

In the prologue to *Social Intelligence*—one of four books on emotional intelligence by Daniel Goleman—he cites this real-life incident:

During the early days of the second American invasion of Iraq, a group of soldiers set out for a local mosque to contact the town's chief cleric. Their goal was to ask his help in organizing the distribution of relief supplies. But a mob gathered, fearing the soldiers were coming to arrest their spiritual leader or destroy the mosque, a holy shrine.

Hundreds of devout Muslims surrounded the soldiers, waving their hands in the air and shouting, as they pressed in toward the heavily armed platoon. The commanding officer, Lieutenant Colonel Christopher Hughes, thought fast.

Picking up a loudspeaker, he told his soldiers to "take a knee," meaning to kneel on one knee.

Next he ordered them to point their rifles toward the ground.

Then his order was: "Smile."

At that, the crowd's mood morphed. A few people were still yelling, but most were now smiling in return. A few patted the soldiers on the back as Hughes ordered them to walk slowly away, backward—still smiling.

That quick-witted move was the culmination of a dizzying array of split-second social calculations. Hughes had to read the level of hostility in that crowd and sense what would calm them. He had to bet on the discipline of his men and the strength of their trust in him. And he had to gamble on hitting just the right gesture that would pierce the barriers of language and culture—all culminating in those spur-of-the-moment decisions.[1]

This example of high emotional intelligence in Hughes recalls a parallel example involving Jesus:

Early in the morning he [Jesus] came again to the temple. All the people came to him and he sat down and began to teach them. The scribes and Pharisees brought a woman who had been caught in adultery; and making her stand before all of them, they said to him, "Teacher, this woman was caught in the very act of committing adultery. Now in the law Moses commanded us to stone such women. Now what do you say?" They said this to test him, so that they might have some charge to bring against him. Jesus bent down and wrote with his finger on the ground. When they kept on questioning him, he straightened up and said to them, "Let anyone among you who is without sin be the first to throw a stone at her." And once again he bent down and wrote on the ground. When they heard it, they went away, one by one, beginning with the elders; and Jesus was left alone with the woman standing before him. Jesus straightened up and said to her, "Woman, where are they? Has no one condemned you?" She said "No one, sir." And Jesus said, "Neither do I condemn you. Go your way, and from now on do not sin again." (John 8:2–11)[2]

These are similar, yet unique, situations involving a hostile crowd. It is our suggestion that when asked what should be done with this woman, Jesus stooped to write with his finger on the ground to give him time to figure out how to manage this emotionally charged situation. He does not want to be accused of ignoring the law of Moses.[3] The scribes and Pharisees assume that he is not fully Torah observant and therefore set a trap for him. Jesus expresses no disagreement with the Torah: she should be executed. But he insists that whoever is without sin should follow the Torah and cast the first stone. At this, his opponents melt away, leaving no one to condemn the woman. Jesus, not having been a witness to the adultery, does not condemn her, either. The story portrays Jesus as a very quick thinker, someone able to defuse a situation of potential danger both to the woman and to him.

At the same time, Jesus is portrayed as remarkably sympathetic to a marginalized woman. Throughout his ministry, Jesus was empathic to the plight of women. Women were always somewhere in the background wherever Jesus traveled to heal and to teach. In Luke 8:1–3, we hear:

> Soon afterwards he went on through cities and villages, proclaiming and bringing the good news of the kingdom of God. The twelve were with him, as well as some women who had been cured of evil spirits and infirmities: Mary, called Magdalene, from whom seven demons had gone out, and Joanna, the wife of Herod's steward Chuza, and Susanna, and many others, who provided for them[4] out of their resources.

In all four Gospels, it is women who stood by when Jesus was being crucified, and it was women who came to Jesus tomb on Easter morning. In the resurrection scenes, the risen Jesus first appeared to Mary Magdalene, who then went to tell the disciples of his appearance. That kind of loyalty could only have emerged from women who sensed Jesus' compassion for them and their plight.

If, in the story of the woman caught in adultery, he had voiced disagreement with the law of Moses in this regard, he would have been stoned to death along with the woman. The situation called for significant emotional intelligence to size up the situation and come up with a solution. It would have been self-defeating if he had stood up and tried to stare down the angry crowd. There was no guarantee that his words would rescue this woman and free himself of the accusation against him. It was his best shot, and it worked. In this passage Jesus can be viewed as having great emotional intelligence by the way he defused this angry mob.

ONE

What Is Emotional Intelligence?

After many years consulting with churches (often in conflict) and training church leaders, Roy Oswald, one of the authors of this book, has concluded that "it's all about relationships" between pastor and congregation and among members of the congregation. The more he learned about emotional intelligence, the more he concluded that it is the most powerful tool that exists to help church leaders enhance their relational skills, which really is what emotional intelligence is all about. That is the reason for this book.

The term "emotional intelligence" was first used by two psychologists, Peter Salovey and John Mayer, in an academic journal in 1990.[1] Daniel Goleman later asked permission to use that term in his book, *Emotional Intelligence* (1995), which became a runaway bestseller.[2] In that book, he poses the question of whether emotional intelligence could be more important than IQ. Soon, emotional intelligence, or EQ, became a topic of conversation across the country. It hit the front cover of *Time* magazine[3] and was discussed on many talk shows. *Time* magazine's front cover implied/hinted at this provocative question: Is your EQ more important than your IQ?

Salovey and Mayer defined emotional intelligence as the "ability to monitor one's own and others' emotions, to discriminate among them and to use this information to guide one's thinking and actions."[4] This ability entails five capacities: knowing one's emotions, managing emotions, motivating oneself, recognizing emotions in others, and handling relationships.[5] Salovey and Mayer have a fairly narrow definition of emotional intelligence, and all these tasks relate to individuals' functioning in their relationships with other people. We prefer a somewhat broader definition of emotional intelligence such as that of psychologist and best-selling author Daniel Goleman. Goleman and his Case Western Reserve University colleague Richard Boyatzis identify these emotional competencies:[6]

- Self-awareness (emotional self-awareness)
- Self-management (achievement orientation, adaptability, emotional self-control, positive outlook)
- Social awareness (empathy, organizational awareness)
- Relationship management (conflict management, coach and mentor, influence, inspirational leadership, teamwork)

For the sake of comparison, here is a list of emotional intelligence categories in the widely used EQ-i 2.0-360 survey by Multi-Health Systems, originally developed by Reuven Bar-On and later revised by MHS:[7]

- self-perception (self-regard, self-actualization, emotional self-awareness)
- self-expression (emotional expression, assertiveness, independence)
- interpersonal composite (interpersonal relationships, empathy, social responsibility)
- decision making (problem solving, reality testing, impulse control)
- stress management (flexibility, stress tolerance, optimism)

Goleman was a pioneer in the application of the emotional intelligence model to the workplace, especially to leadership roles in organizations and companies. His follow-ups to *Emotional Intelligence* (1995) include *Working with Emotional Intelligence* (1998), *Primal Leadership* (coauthor, 2002), and *Social Intelligence* (2006). As these titles suggest, Goleman's focus on the practical applications of emotional intelligence will, we think, be helpful not only for business leaders but also for church leaders. Goleman has also been a pioneer in the explicit use of neuroscientific discoveries—the new "brain science"—understanding emotional intelligence and the roles that emotions play in human thinking and behaving. Most recently, in 2012, neuroscientist Richard Davidson teamed up with

Sharon Begley, a popular author on the human sciences, to publish a book titled *The Emotional Life of Your Brain*, which also explains the practical implications of brain research.[8]

Goleman acknowledges that because the concept of emotional intelligence is so new, longitudinal studies have not yet been conducted comparing the predictive power of EQ against IQ in successful workplace performance over an entire career. After examining several hundred business organizations, however, he concluded that "for jobs of all kinds, emotional competencies were twice as prevalent among distinguishing competencies [those that characterize successful leaders] as were technical skills and purely cognitive abilities combined."[9] Translation: The emotional competencies of pastors and church leaders are probably the most important factors in pastoral effectiveness.

Goleman asserts that IQ is a better threshold competence, but EQ is a better distinguishing competence. That is, IQ may get you into a job, but EQ is needed to perform at the highest level.

Consider a study of eighty-one valedictorians from the 1981 high school classes in Illinois. They were, of course, the brightest students in terms of grade-point average in their respective schools. "But while they continued to achieve well in college, getting excellent grades, by their late twenties" they had attained "only average levels of success. Ten years after graduating from high school, only one in four was at the highest level of young people of comparable age in their chosen professions, and many were doing much less well."[10] The study does not pinpoint the reasons for this, but it suggests that factors other than simple academic performance are necessary to explain the findings. "Academic intelligence offers virtually no preparation for the turmoil—or opportunity—life's vicissitudes bring."[11]

Although longitudinal studies are not available, researchers have been able to explore the role of EQ in a variety of situations, primarily in the business world.[12] One study of the relationship between emotional intelligence and on-the-job performance—said to be the first of its kind—was commissioned by the U.S. Air Force. The study found a strong correlation between seven key EQ traits (social responsibility, assertiveness, interpersonal relationships, empathy, happiness, stress tolerance, and problem solving) and a person's ability to successfully recruit people for the air force. By contrast, factors such as the geographical location of recruiters, their gender, ethnicity, education, age, or hours worked did not predict high or low performance. This led the air force to use emotional intelligence criteria in the selection and training of recruiters. The results were quite dramatic, both increasing productivity and saving money by not replacing recruiters as often.[13]

Subsequent research has supported claims about the positive correlation between EQ and effective leadership. It has been found that the CEO of a company generally sets the emotional tone for the whole corporation. People working for a boss with high emotional intelligence generally do better work, feel more positive about the company, and will go the extra mile to ensure that the company succeeds. Such research suggests that increasing the emotional intelligence of pastors would have a dramatic and positive effect on them and their congregations.

Every model of emotional intelligence begins with the need for self-awareness. Roy has found that many people, including some in church leadership positions, are out of touch with their own emotions. What we are not aware of we cannot control. The very definition of emotional intelligence is the ability to control one's emotions—not to put a damper on them, but to be able to use emotions constructively to achieve desired goals and to form strong, positive relationships. Unfortunately, few rigorous studies of pastoral leadership and congregational effectiveness in relation to emotional competencies have been done, though, in chapters 10 and 11, Roy will discuss the characteristics of the emotionally intelligent congregation and the emotionally intelligent pastor, respectively. His workshops on emotional intelligence for pastors have yielded important insights into how pastors can improve their EQ and thus transform their relationships in their congregations.

There is good reason for the potency of our emotional brain. When we experience a crisis, the emotional brain takes over and commandeers possible action. This is the role of the amygdala within the emotional brain; it stores every frightening experience we have ever had. When the amygdala senses something similar happening to us, it alerts us to the possibility of fight, flight, or freeze. This function of the brain has enabled our survival as a species through thousands of years. We would not be around as a species if we didn't have an amygdala to prepare us for the many hostile situations that we encounter.

To ensure that the amygdala does not continually hijack our brain so that we are in a constant state of flight or fight, however, we have two highly developed prefrontal lobes, which act to moderate those thoughts and feelings. These prefrontal lobes act as an executive center for the brain by receiving information from all parts of the brain so that we can make the decision about what we are to do. If, for example, while strolling through a park as an adult I see a big black dog coming toward me, my amygdala may remember that I was bitten by a big black dog as a child. I may find myself panicking and in a cold sweat. Yet, after a few seconds, I realize that this black dog is different from the one that bit me as child. The prefrontal area of my brain was able to veto an emotional impulse and thus ensure a more effective response. However, if the prefrontal lobes are not able to make this distinction, the amygdala will hijack my brain, and I will completely lose my ability to think clearly and rationally. It will flood my brain with serotonin, and I will move into a flight/flight/freeze mode. Generally the prefrontal lobes have about six seconds to determine whether we are in a genuine crisis or not.

An example of amygdala hijack is when someone stands up in a crowd to make an announcement or speech and experiences stage fright, placing her in panic mode. What emerges may be something completely incoherent and off base.

People who are easily excited may have underdeveloped prefrontal lobes or hyperactive amygdalae. We would say that they lacked the emotional intelligence to deal with the many frightening things that come their way. It is for this reason that we say that our EQ involves managing ourselves and our emotions.

There are other times, however, when these immediate impressions need to be taken more seriously. Daniel Goleman, in one of his CD recordings of interviews with neurological specialists and researchers, talks about a border guard at the Canadian border who was processing people coming into the United States. When a certain male appeared in front of her counter, she sensed that he was highly annoyed at having to go through this inspection process. She excused herself and went back to the office where she asked people to look more carefully into this person's identity. They soon discovered that he was a terrorist and should be apprehended. Her instincts paid off. Her immediate reaction to this man was right on target.

The Brain Science Basis for Emotional Intelligence

We think of emotional intelligence as the practical application of remarkable discoveries in brain science during the last several decades. We need to be clear that we are not experts in either brain science or emotional intelligence, and we are only too aware that this is a rapidly changing field, so we focus on generally accepted views as well as the latest research. Given that disclaimer, however, we believe that arguably the single most important discovery in brain science (or neuroscience) has been the discovery of the role and importance of emotion in human thought and behavior. For centuries in the West, emotion was seen mainly as a distorting factor in reasoning, although there have been times, such as the Romantic Period, when emotion was emphasized. Previously, combining the terms "emotional" and "intelligence" would have seemed like an oxymoron. That these terms can be credibly linked has been supported by extensive research into the role of emotion in brain function and human behavior. We accept the view that emotions are bodily reactions to external stimuli, while feelings are the subjective interpretation of those emotions. For example, our body will react almost instantly to something that endangers us, such as a ball thrown directly at our head. Emotion is the name for the body's response to this. Feeling is our interpretation of our body's response; the feeling is fear.

Charles Darwin was the pioneer in the study of emotions. His book *The Expression of the Emotions in Man and Animals* (1872) called attention to the continuity of emotional expression between animals and humans, including humans in various cultures. The theoretical framework he employed remains crucial today—emotional expression has evolved and emotions need to be understood in terms of their survival value. It is very easy to understand the survival function, for example, of fear, but we need to think about the role of emotions not only for sheer survival but also for flourishing. Joy is a sign of flourishing. There is today an active field of evolutionary psychology based on Darwin's insights. Some important work regarding emotions, such as that of William James,[14] occurred after Darwin. During the heyday of behaviorism, however, emotions were ignored.

The appreciation in modern brain science for the role of emotion in thought and behavior emerged in the second half of the twentieth century, especially in the later decades, when technological advances enabled scientists to conduct noninvasive studies of living brains engaged in various ingenious experiments, to identify which part of the brain did what and how signals passed through the brain's billions of neurons. Another approach—the study of people with severe damage to their brains—also highlighted the importance of emotion in cognition and behavior.

Consider this example: A once-prominent businessman in his thirties developed a life-threatening tumor in his prefrontal lobes. The surgery that removed it was said to be successful, but "Elliot" (the name given him by Antonio Damasio, the researcher) became a changed person following that surgery.[15] He could no longer hold a job. His wife left him. He squandered his savings in fruitless investments and was reduced to living in a spare bedroom in his brother's house.

There was a puzzling pattern to his problem. Intellectually, he was as bright as ever. There was nothing wrong with his logic, memory, attention, or any other cognitive function. He was, however, oblivious of his emotions. He could talk about the tragedy of his experience dispassionately and simply remain objective about it. The surgeon had removed damaged tissue in the right prefrontal lobe; the left side was mostly undamaged. When confronted with a choice, he could give you all the reasons for and against a decision, but he could not decide. He simply could not place a value on one side of the situation or the other. In fact, "Elliot" admitted that pictures that used to evoke strong emotion no longer caused any reaction, positive or negative.

Damasio uses the above case among others to argue that emotion or feeling and thinking (the processing of information by the brain, both consciously and unconsciously) are inseparable parts of our cognitive system. Feelings tell us what is going on in our bodies and, according to Damasio, *"feelings are just as cognitive as any other perceptual image."*[16] This finding refutes the common assumption that emotion and cognition are separate and opposing elements in the human animal. Since feelings are *interpretations* of emotional processes, they deserve to be described as thoughts, as cognition. So emotion and thinking, which for centuries were seen as opposing forces, like horses hitched together but determined to go in opposite directions, are now seen as a functional unity.

Another assumption that has been overturned is that as we age, our brains lose function and that's it—nothing can be done.[17] Not so! Even into old age, the brain can continue to develop, even though some function may be lost. Psychiatrist Norman Doidge traveled the country tracking down stories of remarkable recoveries that individuals have been able to make from various health problems. These stories are collected in his book, *The Brain That Changes Itself: Stories of Personal Triumph from the Frontiers of Brain Science.*[18] Indeed, the fact that you are reading these words means that your brain has already been rewired. According to Maryanne Wolf, "Reading can be learned only because of the brain's plastic design, and when reading takes place, that individual brain is forever changed, both physiologically and intellectually."[19]

Without the discovery of the plasticity of the brain, the whole field of emotional intelligence would not exist. Because of the brain's plasticity, it is possible to change behaviors and attitudes, enhance positive emotions and diminish negative emotions, and thus to actually change the brain itself. All kinds of training programs now exist to enhance people's emotional competencies, and this is done without psychotropic drugs or surgical interventions.

The plasticity of the brain means that our emotional intelligence can be developed, deficiencies corrected, and dysfunctional behaviors altered. EQ training and consulting have grown rapidly in this country. However, EQ training is challenging, because it must go beyond learning the theory of EQ to experiencing accurate *feedback* about the strengths and weaknesses of one's emotional intelligence, assimilating this information, and learning to make needed changes in behavior and attitude. In his experience leading EQ workshops, Roy has found that real growth in emotional intelligence happens best in expertly led small groups, meeting over a period of at least several days, where participants are offered feedback on the impact their words and behavior have on others. However, there are other ways of enhancing one's emotional intelligence, too, such as hiring a coach trained in EQ, or organizing a peer group committed to this task and led by a trained facilitator.

We need to stress that increasing one's EQ is not easy. It takes hard work over a long period of time. But consider how enriched congregations are when they are led by emotionally intelligent, spiritually mature leaders. These are communities of healing, vital places where exciting things are going on, where mission and ministry are being realized. An emotionally intelligent leader is a nonanxious presence in the midst of sometimes infantile congregational behaviors, able to deal with the inevitable conflicts that arise in parish life. And a pastor who improves his emotional intelligence will find that his ministry is more fulfilling and effective, less draining and frustrating. Even if a congregation does not provide EQ training for its pastor and other leaders, the pastor or pastors might take the initiative and seek this training as part of their continuing education.

Conclusion

We hope that readers will find emotional intelligence a fascinating and useful field with many applications in church life. In subsequent chapters, we will examine in greater depth some of the key traits of an emotionally intelligent person. Then we will explore two key questions: What is an emotionally intelligent pastor or church leader? What is an emotionally intelligent congregation?

TWO

The Emotional Intelligence of Jesus

This is a book about the importance of emotional intelligence in the culture and dynamics of congregational life, with Jesus as the exemplar. Our hope is that viewing Jesus through the lens of emotional intelligence will actually advance our understanding of Jesus. Not only that, it will also bring out dimensions of emotional intelligence that are not the focus of emotional intelligence literature but are central to the Way, the path Jesus invites us to travel. We can imagine pastors preaching the Gospel texts in a new way, sharing the very practical insights to be gained by viewing Jesus through a different lens. We believe that readers will discover that emotional intelligence is not a secular agenda or a language foreign to the church; rather, Jesus himself exemplifies it. At the same time, we do not want to turn Jesus into a puppet voicing our own ideas.

The discerning reader will wonder: How can the authors know anything about Jesus' emotional intelligence? That's a very good question, and the reader has a right to hear our answer to this question. We are, after all, claiming to talk about "the emotional intelligence *of* Jesus." Are we justified in claiming to know anything about Jesus' emotional intelligence?

Though we are aware that we cannot peer into the mind and soul of Jesus, the Gospels can inform us about Jesus' emotional intelligence.

There are several ways we can legitimately assess the emotional intelligence of Jesus. First, we can examine a few explicit statements in the Gospels about Jesus' emotional states (e.g., that he had compassion). Second, we can make inferences from sayings of Jesus about assumptions or views he held. For example, Jesus' saying about taking the log out of your own eye before you try to take the speck out of your neighbor's eye (Matthew 7:3–5) clearly indicates that Jesus understood the need for self-awareness. Third, we can make claims about Jesus as he is portrayed in Gospel accounts. In this case, we are doing the same thing that Shakespeare scholars might do with a character such as Hamlet. Whether these portraits of Jesus in the Gospels are historically accurate is not our concern, because we are making claims only about Jesus as a literary character in the Gospels. Fourth, and in some ways the most interesting, we can explore the emotional intelligence implicit in Jesus' admonitions. For example, what kind of emotional intelligence would be required to love one's enemies or to forgive without limit? In fact, we believe that careful attention to Jesus' sayings about forgiveness and love of enemies is of special importance. These reflect a profound understanding of human nature that can be articulated in terms of emotional intelligence.

The only sources of information about Jesus that we will use are the four Gospels. These accounts, especially the first three,[1] have some of the characteristics of a biography, in that they tell stories about Jesus, but they are not biographies in the modern sense. They ignore Jesus' early life, lack any description of what Jesus looked like, provide only scant information about his family and basically no information about his education or training, and only occasionally mention his motivations. For the most part, the Gospels ignore Jesus' first thirty years. No modern biographer would do that. More importantly, the Gospels are "gospel"—"good news," the proclamation of a religious message. Given their special character as proclamation rather than biography, we must be careful when making assertions about Jesus' emotional intelligence.

The Emotional Jesus

Jesus, of course, was emotional simply because he was human. But our concern is not whether or not Jesus experienced emotion. Emotional intelligence has to do with what we do with our emotions. Are we aware of our own emotions? Are we able to control them? Are we aware of the emotional states of those around us?

The Gospels actually do mention some emotional states of Jesus. In general, a survey of the texts shows that positive emotions such as love and pity, compassion, or mercy predominate, and Jesus is portrayed as controlling his fears and worries. Negative emotions are rarely ascribed to Jesus, and he is said to warn against anger, greed, lust, worry, fear, and hatred. Sometimes incidents, such as the cursing of the fig tree (Mark 11:12–14) and the so-called "cleansing" of the Temple (Mark 11:15–18 and parallels), are cited as examples of Jesus' anger, but these Gospel accounts lack any reference to Jesus' emotional state.

We do hear of Jesus loving a rich young man (Mark 10:21), Martha and her sister (John 11:5), Lazarus (John 11:36), and an unnamed disciple (John 19:26; 20:2; 21:7, 20). In the Gethsemane scene, Jesus is said to be distressed, agitated, and grieved (Mark 14:32–34). Jesus "eagerly desired" to be with his disciples at the Last Supper (Luke 22:15). Only once is Jesus said to have been angry (Mark 3:5, where his anger is directed at his opponents). However, Jesus also demanded that his followers control their anger (Matthew 5:22), and there are numerous injunctions to love the neighbor, and even the enemy.

Jesus is generally portrayed as having no fear, as when a storm comes up on the Sea of Galilee and he is found asleep in the storm-tossed boat (Mark 4:38). Even though he was warned that Herod Antipas was seeking to kill him, he insisted on continuing his work (Luke 13:31–32). He warned his followers repeatedly not to fear those who could do them harm and told them to have no anxiety about anything, even—since they apparently depended on begging for a living—about what to eat or what to wear (Luke 12:22/Matthew 6:25).

Jesus is portrayed as having compassion or mercy, especially on the sick (e.g., Mark 6:34; 8:2), and he says that those who show mercy are blessed (Matthew 5:7). After he sees Mary weeping over the death of Lazarus, Jesus also weeps (John 11:35). He also wept over the city of Jerusalem (Luke 19:41).

While we need to be cautious about taking these statements about Jesus' emotional states as grist for psychological analysis, the portrait of Jesus in the Gospels is remarkably consistent: he eschewed negative emotions such as fear, anger, and hatred, and he displayed as well as demanded only positive emotions. This simple survey of statements in the Gospels about Jesus' emotional reactions thus suggests that Jesus, at least as portrayed in the Gospels, possessed the kind of emotional intelligence described elsewhere in this book.

Still, is it really credible to claim that Jesus was the very epitome of emotional intelligence? After all, critics of Jesus find his claims about himself exaggerated, if not preposterous, a sign of megalomania. His own family is said to have considered him crazy (Mark 3:21), while the scribes said he was demon possessed (Mark 3:22). Jesus' negative treatment of his own family and his demands that followers abandon their families could be understood to reflect the kind of dysfunctional family situation that would produce a maladjusted son. Others have claimed he was subject to hallucinations or delusions of grandeur.

Such accusations were faced by Albert Schweitzer in the dissertation he wrote for his medical degree, which addressed psychological assessments such as those mentioned. In *The Psychiatric Study of Jesus*,[2] Schweitzer faulted such assessments both for psychological naïveté and for an uncritical approach to the Gospels, setting a precedent for critical analysis of psychological diagnoses of Jesus. The Fourth Gospel, he pointed out, is lightly regarded as a source for the historical Jesus, as is still the case. That Gospel contains many of the extravagant claims on which psychological assessments of Jesus are often made. Scholars relying on the historical critical method, such as Rudolf Bultmann, the Jesus Seminar, and many others, believe Jesus' messianic claims were placed on his lips by the early church. Our assessment of Jesus' emotional intelligence is based primarily on the synoptic tradition (Matthew, Mark, and Luke), which is widely regarded as the most reliable source for Jesus' teaching. This book is not the place to defend these judgments at the length that would be required.

Jesus the Barefoot Doctor

We believe Jesus' healings are strong evidence for Jesus' emotional intelligence. The Gospels often attribute healings to the ill person's "faith" or trust in Jesus. "Your faith has made you well" is attributed to Jesus numerous times. There must have been something about this faith or trust that was able to bring about dramatic physical change in the bodies of ill persons. Since Jesus is portrayed as an exceptional healer, it seems fair to conclude that he had an unusual capacity for eliciting healing trust in ill persons. We regard this as evidence of emotional intelligence. Since this is such a crucial point, we need to develop it at some length.

The Gospels portray Jesus as gaining popularity on the basis of both his teaching and his healing, especially the latter. We need only follow the opening chapters of the Gospel of Mark to see this. At the beginning of his ministry, he is in Capernaum and exorcises a demon, and "at once his fame began to spread throughout the surrounding region of Galilee" (Mark 1:28). Then he heals Peter's mother-in-law of a fever, and at sundown word has spread so "all who were sick or possessed with demons" come to him (Mark 1:32). In the morning, he seeks a secluded place, but Simon and his companions find him and tell him, "Everyone is searching for you" (Mark 1:37). The same story repeats itself over and over in all the synoptics.[3] Healing clearly was something for which there seems to have been a great, unfulfilled need. The ability to elicit healing trust apparently distinguished Jesus from others and was the basis for his popularity, perhaps an authenticating sign that he was a holy man or shaman.[4] We regard these healings as "psychosomatic," to use older terminology, requiring a deep connection between the healer and the healed. We will discuss this at greater length shortly.

If we wish to understand what Jesus' healings were about, we need to try to understand the mind-set of the people in Jesus' day. This means setting aside, to the extent that we can, our modern assumptions about disease, health, and healing, many of which we are not even aware of. We must enter into that dark, strange world of demons and gods and "doctors" who today would likely be regarded as quacks. Yet we will see that we are not really all that different from people in these "primitive" societies.

Quite likely, the Gospel writers piously thought it their duty to make the stories of Jesus' healings even more remarkable and inspiring than they were. On the other hand, most critical scholars assume that he actually did heal people . . . somehow. There are just too many stories of healing to dismiss them all as fabrications. Even members of the skeptical Jesus Seminar (of which Arland Jacobson, the other author of this book, was a member) agreed that Jesus performed miracles.[5] How they happened, how they are to be interpreted, and whether they imply Jesus' possession of some divine power are completely separate questions.

Sickness was common in Jesus' day. Sanitation was poor. Except in the fancy homes of the wealthy elites, running water and sewerage were unknown. As we will see later, there probably were no wealthy elites in Capernaum. Life was usually short. Many died in childbirth (mother and child) or infancy, and there were all kinds of tensions and stresses within families as a result of poverty and poor living conditions. Many people in Jesus' day were very poor subsistence farmers or, around the Sea of Galilee, subsistence fishermen, often in debt, and thus also under great stress.

Especially important was the impact of urbanization under Herod Antipas, who ruled from 4 BC to AD 20. Antipas built two urban centers, Tiberias and then Sepphoris, the first relatively sizable cities in Galilee. The need to feed the residents of these cities resulted in a transition from traditional to commercial agriculture, as a result of which peasants lost their land and went into debt, resulting in growing poverty, malnutrition, the disruption of village life, and dramatic income inequality between urban elites and an impoverished peasantry.[6]

Everyone in Jesus' day lived in a world radically different from the bright and sterile world of modern medicine. We know about germs and viruses; they did not. We have a growing understanding of the brain, hormones, circulatory and endocrine systems, and much more, none of which was known then. One theory in those days was that illness was the result of sins committed by the sick person or his parents. Once Jesus was asked, "Who sinned, this man or his parents, that he was born blind?" (John 9:2; cf. Luke 13:1–5). At times, Jesus seems to reject the "sin theory" of disease, but at other times, he forgives the ill person, and this seems to have been a critical factor in healing. Another theory of the era was that illness was caused by demon possession. Jesus "rebuked the unclean spirit" of a boy (Mark 9:25), a demon came out, and he was healed. Many of Jesus' healings are said to have come about through the expulsion of demons. Jews believed that God was the ultimate source of healing, though folk healers or so-called physicians might help.[7] By our standards, these physicians knew very little, and their effectiveness was sometimes questioned. For example, the woman with an abnormal flow of menstrual blood had gone for twelve years to many different physicians, had spent all her money, had suffered greatly from their "treatments," and had experienced no improvement (Mark 5:25–34). But her trust in Jesus as healer had been kindled by reports she had heard about Jesus (Mark 5:27–28). Her condition made her socially isolated, since her uncontrolled bleeding would have made associating with her taboo; healing would have also restored her to her community.[8] Her isolation is evident in the fact that she felt it necessary to try to sneak up on Jesus. But her trust in Jesus is affirmed by him: "Your faith has made you well" (Mark 5:34).

Scholars have realized only in the past few decades that understanding life and sickness in rural first-century Galilee requires setting aside our modern ideas and turning to medical anthropologists who study more "primitive" societies, similar to those in Jesus' day. One of the pioneers in this approach has been Catholic biblical scholar John Pilch, whose work has been collected in his book *Healing in the New Testament: Insights from Medical and Mediterranean Anthropology.*[9] Pilch sees Jesus as a folk healer, using touch (Mark 1:41), spittle (Mark 8:23), and mud (John 9:6), as well as powerful words (Mark 5:41; 7:34), to heal. But he especially emphasizes that "healing" and "disease" are interpretive concepts that embody cultural values and assumptions. For example, when we say someone is "sick," we assume some biomedical condition, not a condition resulting from demons or sin.

Spanish biblical scholar Santiago Guijarro lists three of the main differences between modern scientific and ancient understandings of illness and healing.[10] First, in prescientific cultures, people do not separate the spheres of the natural, the supernatural, society, and the individual. Second, the healer participates in and depends upon the value systems and understandings of his culture, and these differ sharply from modern assumptions and values. Third, healing is less individual than communal, involving not just the ill person but also that person's family and community. Pilch, in fact, stresses healing as a "meaning-restoring" process in which a person who has been excluded from his community by his illness is restored to that community and to normal functions within it. For example, the demoniac who had to leave the city of the living to dwell in the city of the dead was restored to his community (Mark 5:1–16).

An analysis of Jesus as shaman is, we believe, even more helpful than such anthropological approaches, though this approach has much in common with those. University of South Africa scholar Pieter F. Craffert argues at some length about the need to break from the "biomedical" model, which separates body and mind, and assumes that different regimens are required for healing the body and healing the mind.[11] He instead speaks of a "biopsychosocial" paradigm, a term used by some medical anthropologists. And he uses the ancient tradition of the shaman or holy man as a model for understanding Jesus' healing. There was a constellation of cultural beliefs and practices associated with the holy man or shaman, and these cultural beliefs and practices were, and are, basic to healing by shamans.

As Craffert points out, the artificiality of the body-mind dualism can be seen in the placebo effect, where in study after study, it turns out that placebos are often just as efficacious as "real" pills. Placebos work within a specific cultural context, one in which there is a widespread set of beliefs associated with the efficacy of pills. For example, studies show that a branded placebo is more effective than a nonbranded placebo. A placebo administered by a doctor is more effective than a sugar pill shared by a friend. Illness and healing, therefore, are at least in part cultural, not simply medical, phenomena. In the ancient world, touching, the application of mud or saliva, the use of magical words (e.g., *talitha kumi* in Mark 5:41 or *ephphatha* in Mark 7:34), and the use of exorcism were all associated with traditional healers, and there is no reason to believe they did not work, just as placebos can work in our culture.

In addition to cultural beliefs and practices, however, one other factor is needed for healing to occur. There must be a figure who can manipulate those beliefs and practices, or who at least has a reputation for being able to do that. In our culture, a mystique surrounds the doctor: tales of the rigor of medical school, the white coat, the diplomas on the wall, a system that limits access to the doctor, scientific apparatuses and environment—all these create an expectation that the doctor has skills, knowledge, and abilities to deal with disease. Like modern healers, the traditional healer also had to have gained a reputation for healing, a reputation based on his entire manner, his actions, and his teachings. For example, consider this account in Matthew 4:23–25:

> Jesus went throughout Galilee, teaching in their synagogues and proclaiming the good news of the kingdom and curing every disease and every sickness among the people. So his fame spread throughout all Syria, and they brought to him all the sick, those who were afflicted with various diseases and pains, demoniacs, epileptics, and paralytics, and he cured them. And great crowds followed him from Galilee, the Decapolis, Jerusalem, Judea, and from beyond the Jordan.

It was this fame that enabled Jesus to be an effective healer. The factors that went into creating this fame are elusive; we can't really know what they were. Since trust in the healer was essential for healing, however, we believe that Jesus must have had the capacity to elicit faith in ill persons. We believe that Jesus had what is sometimes called "resonance" with people, an ability to communicate deeply and effectively, to awaken trust in them. Perhaps his transgression of cultic boundaries and association with the marginalized also inspired confidence among the poor and ill. We suggest this capacity to elicit trust can be characterized as a form of emotional intelligence, because emotional intelligence is a cluster of skills or traits that enable significant relationships.

In fact, modern psychiatric theory allows us to be even more specific about how the diseases that Jesus healed might be understood. It is important to notice several things about Jesus' healings. First, as we noted above, the healings are commonly attributed to the "faith" of the subject of the healing, sometimes accompanied by touch and/or by some medium (e.g., saliva, mud). Thus, at least some of the healings could be described as "relational events," requiring interaction between Jesus and the ill person. Second, the healings are usually instantaneous. For example, a paralyzed man is told to pick up his mat and go. Third, certain kinds of healings predominate, including blindness, deafness, epilepsy, "leprosy,"[12] and paralysis.

Misericordia University professor Stevan L. Davies apparently was the first to propose a specific psychological explanation for Jesus' healing miracles.[13] They were, he argued, cases of "conversion disorder" or "somatization disorder," which are two versions of the general category of "somatoform disorders," now lumped together under the category of "somatic symptom disorders" (SSD) in *Diagnostic and Statistical Manual of Mental Disorders (DSM-5)* (2013).[14] These disorders are typically temporary, although persistent conditions may occur in which a motor or sensory function is lost but no physical or nutritional cause can be identified. The person is not faking it. Common symptoms of SSD include deafness, blindness, numbness, paralysis, and fits—that is, the kinds of illnesses Jesus treated. The acquired condition is certainly real, but it lacks a specific medical cause. Since no physical cause would be involved, the blind person would have the physical potential to see, the deaf person to hear, the paralyzed person to walk, and so on.

One condition that aids recovery in modern cases of these disorders is simply a supportive relationship between the patient and the caregiver. This is where Craffert's discussion of "doctor as drug" is especially relevant.[15] Citing a variety of cases, Craffert says:

> With confidence in the doctor, patients who received sham surgery to treat arthritis of the knee reported relief; patients treated by a sympathetic doctor need fewer narcotics to do the same job; patients recover more quickly if they believe the doctor is in control; drugs are more effective when healers believe in their efficiency.[16]

Craffert's point about the "doctor as drug" helps erase the distance between the "primitive" healing of Jesus and certain instances of healing today. We know that the body is quite capable of healing itself and often does so. With the added component of faith in the healer, the body surely could heal itself. We are not fundamentally different from "primitive" people. The difference is that we operate with a very different set of cultural symbols and understandings. Faith is as important to our medical system as it was in the understandings of illness and healing in Jesus' day.

To return to somatic disorders, while they are not fully understood, most experts agree that they result from some traumatic situation or some emotional problem that gets unconsciously "converted" into a bodily symptom. The subject gains some kind of relief from this problem, even if the result is being disabled in some way. Two kinds of gains are usually identified. The "primary gain" is interior—namely, relief from serious emotional trauma. It may be easier to deal with deafness, for example, than the psychic pain of rejection. There can also be a "secondary gain." For example, a person might be trapped in an intolerable family or village situation and might incur a physical disorder that exempts that person from overwhelmingly stressful expectations placed on her. This, in fact, might have been the case with the woman with the menstrual hemorrhage in Mark 5. We can only speculate, but perhaps the woman's illness allowed her to escape a bad marriage. Princeton theologian Donald Capps has explored this case and others in greater detail using the somatic disorder theory.[17]

Somatoform disorders are generally more common in rural, lower socioeconomic groups. This would certainly fit our picture of first-century Galilee, where in addition there would be highly patriarchal, close-knit families, in which there would be no easy escape from or remedy for emotional trauma. In such circumstances, it would hardly be unusual for somatic disorders to be fairly common.

Jesus is often said to attribute healings to faith, but there is another theory also found in the Gospels. In several cases, the Gospels attribute Jesus' exorcism or healing ability to *exousia*, "authority" (e.g., Mark 1:27; 3:15; Luke 7:8). In the Gospels, *exousia* always implies authorization by some external source. It is not an inherent quality, a charisma. In the case of Jesus, the implied authorization is from God (e.g., Mark 11:28–33). Jesus' *exousia* was seen as extraordinary, not like that of the scribes (Mark 1:22; Matthew 7:29). In addition, Jesus could grant this authority to others, as in Mark 1:27, where Jesus gives his disciples the authority to cast out demons. In fact, it is in exorcisms that this authority is most clearly expressed: Jesus simply commands the demons to depart, and they leave.

Healings attributed to touch (e.g., Mark 3:10; 6:56), on the other hand, would seem to indicate an inherent ability or power. As we have seen, the frequent attribution of healings to the "faith" of the ill person in Jesus as healer provides still a different understanding of the healing process. Thus, the Gospels offer several understandings of how Jesus was able to heal: divine authorization, special power, and the faith of the one healed. These are not necessarily mutually exclusive understandings. But without the faith of the "patients," the healer could not heal, despite the power of his touch and his divine authorization, as we see in Mark 6:5–6, where Jesus was unable to heal many. In other words, healings occurred when Jesus was able to evoke or elicit "faith" or trust in the ill person. This is a relational skill that could broadly be described as emotional intelligence, combining empathy and inspiration, both of which will be discussed more fully later.

Jesus, Believer in Abundance

As we saw, the EQ traits of empathy and inspiration were key to Jesus' healings, eliciting the trust of the ill person in the healer. Another EQ trait that we find in Jesus is what might be called optimism, though it is a special kind of optimism.

In 1965, anthropologist George Foster published his classic article "Peasant Society and the Image of Limited Good."[18] Foster developed a model for the functioning of peasant society from his study of a community in Mexico (Tzintzuntzan), but understood it as a model applicable generally to peasant societies. He sought to identify the "cognitive orientation" of peasant society, an orientation that would not be articulated but would subsume the greatest amount of behaviors in the society. This cognitive orientation could explain and predict peasant behaviors, and also help identify why peasant societies fail to make economic progress. He called this cognitive orientation the "image of limited good," which means a zero-sum mentality: there is only so much of any good, whether material or other, so whenever one person acquires some good, another person is deprived of it. Thus, he observed that "broad areas of peasant behavior are patterned in such fashion as to suggest that peasants view their social, economic, and natural universes—their total environment—as one in which all of the desired things in life such as land, wealth, health, friendship and love, manliness and honor, respect and status, power and influence, security and safety, *exist in finite quantity* and *are always in short supply.*"

Moreover, "there is no way directly within peasant power to increase specific quantities."[19] This assumption of limited good has a leveling and antiprogressive tendency. For someone to stand out and assert himself would be seen as depriving others of status and influence. This image actually accords with peasant reality. Foster notes that someone with this mentality "is usually very near the truth"[20]—namely, that good things really are scarce in a peasant society. This makes a peasant society very conservative, prizing security and stability rather than change.

A recent study of scarcity by a Harvard economist and a Princeton psychologist, both of whom study poverty and the poor, arrived at similar conclusions (though without reference to Foster's work). Perceived scarcity, they found, has profound and similar effects whether the scarcity is of time, money, food, friends, or most anything.[21] The effects can be positive, as when a scarcity of time (e.g., imminent deadlines) can concentrate the mind, produce results, and yield better time management. But this same concentration can produce a psychological tunnel vision, short-term thinking, and diminished impulse control (e.g., dieters may lack ability to resist food temptation because their attention is so focused on food). They discovered, by testing farmers who depend on a once-a-year harvest payoff, that scarcity can literally lower a person's IQ. The IQ of such farmers after the harvest registered a significant gain over their preharvest IQ. The perception of scarcity, these researchers believe, is relative and produces a psychology of scarcity that leads the poor to adopt behaviors that are unhelpful, including neglecting tasks that would ensure better crops, failing to follow a medical regimen, taking high-interest loans, and so on.

Capernaum, Jesus' hometown, was a peasant village. The images and metaphors in the Gospels reflect a peasant agrarian society, with fields, crops, birds, indebted farmers, and a sharp contrast between the local poor and the distant rich. Archaeologists have found no elite structures— villas, paved streets, elaborate public structures, water systems—in this small town on the north shore of the Sea of Galilee.[22] Such structures existed in the newly Romanized towns of Tiberias and Sepphoris not far away, but Jesus apparently never went to those cities. Rather, he lived in a world of scarcity—a poor Jewish village.[23] The people with whom he dealt had little and little hope of getting more. Life was a day-to-day struggle. Some of Capernaum's peasants farmed small plots nearby, while others fished for a living, which also seems not to have been a very prosperous endeavor.[24] (A first-century fishing boat discovered not far from Capernaum, in 1986 when the lake was low, had been repeatedly repaired using inferior woods.)[25] Theirs was a world of "can't," not "can."

People with a scarcity mentality focus on limits, are able to see only their immediate needs, are fearful of loss, have diminished impulse control, focus on the short term, and see themselves in competition for scarce resources. People with an abundance mentality, on the other hand, focus on possibilities and are willing to take risks. Scarcity thinkers tend to be resentful of the success of others. They are into hoarding, into defending what they have. Abundance thinkers are generous, willing to share what they have. They have confidence that there will be enough for everyone.

Jesus had an abundance mentality and challenged his followers to adopt this mentality. Abundance thinking differs from conventional views of optimism, because it is a view of the world grounded in confidence in God's graciousness and generosity ("Ask, and you will receive!"); it is not simply belief that things are good and will be well in the future. Nor does Jesus' abundance mentality resemble the modern "gospel of prosperity" preached by some in the United States. It had nothing to do with getting rich. It was all about God providing enough—a gospel of sufficiency. God provides what we need, not necessarily what we want.

In a world of scarcity, Jesus preached abundance. He told his followers, who had to beg for their daily food and lodging, not to worry about their food or clothing but to trust that God would provide what they would need (Luke 12:22–30/Matthew 6:25–32). The feeding of the multitudes was a demonstration of abundance (Mark 6:30–44/Matthew 14:13–21/Luke 9:12–17/John 6:1–15 and Mark 8:1–10/Matthew 15:32–39). The disciples wonder how it will be possible to feed such a huge multitude with a paltry two dried fishes and five pita breads. Not only is there enough for the multitude, but food is also left over, enough to feed still more.

In the Lord's Prayer, Jesus taught us to pray for "our daily bread"— that is, enough bread for the day, just as the Israelites were commanded to gather only enough manna for the day (Exodus 16:4). Those who gathered more than the daily share found that worms devoured this "more" (Exodus 16:18–20). A rich man whose abundant crops prompted him to build more barns to hoard his surplus is cited as an example of folly (Luke 12:15–21).

Jesus called his disciples to abandon home, family, and property, which was a kind of boot camp in abundance thinking. Having nothing, they would discover that they did not need anything, that their needs would be met, that God would provide. The opposite lifestyle—a life of acquisitiveness—would teach the opposite lesson: namely, to not rely on God to provide. Jesus asked rhetorically, "For what will it profit them [those who seek to save themselves] to gain the whole world and forfeit their life?" (Mark 8:36/Matthew 16:26/Luke 9:25). The saying implies that acquisitiveness is dangerous to one's soul, presumably because it trains one to depend upon self rather than God. That is why "those who want to save their life will lose it" (Mark 8:35/Luke 17:33).

Reflection on the nature of much of Jesus' teachings helps us to grasp how Jesus was able to challenge the image of limited good and the psychology of scarcity. There is a subversive quality to his language that biblical scholar John Dominic Crossan in particular has helped us to grasp in his luminous writings.[26] Jesus' parables could open people's imagination and undermine their assumptions of scarcity and limits. He told them of seeds sown by a farmer that were subject to every sort of difficulty; yet some produced ears bearing dozens, or even more, new seeds—multiplying themselves in amazing abundance (Mark 4:2–9). From a single seed there might develop an ear with ten, twenty, thirty, or more grains of wheat. The parables embody Jesus' experience of a gracious and shocking God, a God whose mind-blowing kingdom violates our normal, everyday worlds in order to break us open to that experience of a gracious God. A very little—a tiny seed (Mark 4:30–32) or a bit of sourdough (Luke 13:20–21)—can have remarkable effect.

We believe an abundance mentality is a sign of emotional intelligence. It is a form of optimism, but it has a special character because it is rooted in confidence in God's care and because it focuses on having enough, on contentment, not on self-centered dreams of unrealistic lavish prosperity. Jesus had been tempted with such promises and rejected them. Jesus' abundance mentality was not just an attitude; it was also a serene, confident trust in God to provide, as God had promised over and over again to God's people. Perhaps the most articulate and passionate modern exponent of an abundance mentality today, and critic of a scarcity mentality, is Walter Brueggemann.[27]

Following Jesus

If, as we claim, Jesus was emotionally intelligent, does it not make sense that following Jesus will result in emotionally intelligent disciples? That, in fact, is what we now wish to claim.

Jesus did not call people to adopt a set of beliefs but a set of practices.[28] Like ancient philosophers, Jesus had disciples who were to listen to his teachings but also observe how Jesus responded to various situations. The Gospels present many anecdotes about Jesus' responses to questions and to situations. The disciples were to learn from these and then become practitioners of the way of life he was teaching. As Jesus said, "A disciple is not above the teacher, but everyone who is fully qualified[29] will be like the teacher" (Luke 6:40). The synoptic Gospels do not portray the many failures and misunderstandings by the disciples to show how obtuse they were, but rather to teach hearers of the Gospels—the secondhand disciples—that discipleship entails a steep learning curve.

It was crucial to live out Jesus' teachings, as he himself did. In the Gospel of Luke's "Sermon on the Plain," Jesus asks, "Why do you call me 'Lord, Lord,' and do not do what I tell you?" (Luke 6:46). This challenge is followed by the famous metaphor of the house built on sand and the house built on rock (Luke 6:47–49). Those who build a house on a rock are those who actually live by the words of Jesus. Discipleship is learned not by studying the theology of Jesus, but by living in the way Jesus taught. Much of the power of this kind of teaching derived from the congruence between his words and his deeds. We speak of this as authenticity. And authenticity is the result of several EQ qualities: transparency, self-awareness, empathy, and inspiration. The product of authenticity is the ability to establish and maintain relationships, to elicit trust and resonance with others. In this additional sense, we believe that Jesus demonstrated emotional intelligence.

Conclusion and Lessons for Congregations

From our examination of the emotional intelligence of Jesus in relation to some key aspects of his ministry, we conclude that emotional intelligence was quite simply key to Jesus' ministry and effectiveness. It was "key" in the sense that without emotional intelligence, Jesus would not have been able to deeply understand the situation of his people or relate to them in such powerful ways.

As a human being, of course, Jesus had emotions. Emotional intelligence has to do with how we manage our emotions so as to function effectively in relationships. The portrait of Jesus, we found, is remarkably consistent: Jesus affirms, displays, and promotes positive emotions such as compassion, and he avoids and warns against negative emotions such as hatred, greed, envy, and fear. Jesus counseled self-awareness (e.g., Matthew 7:3–5). We focused especially on Jesus' healing activity and tried to show how this was possible and how it depended on emotional intelligence. Jesus was seen to be capable of eliciting the healing power of trust, which, we suggested, required empathy and the ability to inspire trust. We argued that Jesus was part of a peasant society, a key characteristic of which is the reality of scarcity, and that Jesus challenged this mentality in both word and action with his abundance mentality, his optimism, rooted in trust in the graciousness and generosity of God. And we noted that Jesus practiced what he preached, that he was therefore perceived as authentic, and that this enabled him to relate in a powerful way with others.

In later chapters, we will address two of the most profound lessons we have to learn from Jesus, both of which go well beyond what we read in the literature of emotional intelligence. These lessons concern forgiveness and love of enemies.

Our examination of Jesus' emotional intelligence suggests some lessons for our churches. First, Jesus clearly had a deep understanding of his people. His was not a disembodied proclamation, but one that responded to the deepest needs of his people. This was possible because of his emotional intelligence. Are our congregations equally sensitive to and responsive to the deepest needs of our people? Second, Jesus did not focus only on his little band of followers; he reached out to all who needed healing, to those isolated, troubled, poor, ill, and stigmatized. He taught his followers by example to do the same. Are our congregations equally focused on training their own to reach out to those who are isolated, troubled, poor, and ill?

THREE

Self-Awareness and Jesus

S elf-awareness is the capacity to identify, moment by moment, the thoughts, emotions, and body sensations occurring within us. It allows us to observe our behavior, both in the past and in the present. While in a conversation with someone, not only are we able to participate in the dialogue taking place, but we can also observe the feelings we are having about the conversation, thoughts we are having about the conversation but are not expressing, our body movements, and possibly what our nonverbal behavior might be saying to this other person. Self-awareness is often called the cornerstone of emotional intelligence, and it distinguishes humans from all other mammals. It is not just the gift of consciousness; it is also being conscious of our own consciousness. Dogs or cats, for example, may be aware of their need for food or protection, but, as far as we know, they are not able to be aware of thoughts they have on the subject.

Research by the Hay Group in Boston showed that people rated low in self-awareness also rated low in other competencies, while those rated high in self-awareness also rated high in a number of other competencies.[1] This indicates that self-awareness is foundational to the development of other competencies, and thus to emotional intelligence in general.

Emotions are internal experiences that impact us. Feelings are our brains' interpretation of those emotions. Often we do not bring these emotions into consciousness. We do not choose to be unaware of these emotions—we simply remain oblivious to them. Strong emotions hit us like a body blow. We do not consciously create them; they simply happen. Self-awareness allows us to become conscious of these emotions and aware of their intensity. Managing those emotions well determines a key part of our emotional intelligence because we cannot manage emotions of which we are not aware. We are able to bring a kind of intelligence to those emotions. In addition to being aware of emotions, we can become aware of the thoughts we have about an experience. With heightened self-awareness, we can observe how thoughts and emotions influence each other and can even shape our thought processes. When, however, we emerge from a school system that values only our thoughts, we can easily come to ignore our emotions.

The analogy of an elephant with a rider can be instructive at this point. Think of emotions as the elephant—strong, powerful, sometimes over-whelming. The role of the rider is not that of guiding the elephant but providing a rationale for why the elephant is doing what it is doing. The analogy breaks down in that there are times when rational thought can change the way we feel about things, but it is usually the other way around.

In the past, some twenty-five-plus years ago, emotions were con-sidered static that got in the way of rational thought. The predominant therapeutic process at the time was rational/emotive therapy or cognitive therapy. The goal of the therapist was to straighten out the thought pro-cesses of the patient, believing that the emotions of the patient would nat-urally fall in line with these better thoughts. This form of therapy would not have lasted as long as it did if it did not produce results. Much of that changed, however, when research on the human brain discovered how much more central emotions are to thoughts. Most therapeutic processes practiced today work primarily with a client's feelings, which, in turn, changes his thought processes.

Emotions and thoughts can distort each other. Each can correct the other. This process can evolve as we grow older. We know that racism, sexism, heterosexism, and other forms of prejudice continue to be major issues in the world. Some people mouth all the right words, but we know that their behavior is not congruent with their thinking. Prejudice is rooted mainly in emotions that continue to distort our thinking on these issues. Caught between thoughts and emotions, which has the best chance of changing the other? Most likely, both need to nudge the other toward a fairer and more accurate assessment of other people, but in millions of cases these prejudices remain stubbornly in place. What seems to have the greatest chance of changing people's perspectives on others is to find a way to come to know some of them personally. When that happens, what changes first, thoughts or emotions? Within heighted self-awareness, we have a chance of watching ourselves change and becoming aware of how we have changed over the years.

Earlier in this book, in chapter 1, we referred to "Elliot," a corporate executive who needed surgery to remove a tumor the size of a small orange.[2] The surgery was deemed successful, but Elliot was not the same after this surgery. Within a short time, his board fired him. Later his wife left him. He could not even hold down a menial job. He was reduced to living in a spare bedroom in his brother's house, having squandered most of his financial resources. Rationally, Elliot was as bright as ever. In conversations, he could provide you with all the reasons for or against a point of view, but he could not decide which would be the better decision. In removing the tumor, surgeons had to remove some of the frontal cortex, which severed the connection between his limbic (emotions) brain and his neocortex. This left him completely devoid of emotions. Without emotions, he could no longer make decisions. Without the ability to integrate thinking and emotion, we can't make decisions that affect real life. We are able to observe many streams of logical thought in our brain, but it is our emotional brain that enables us to decide which options we will choose. Without self-awareness, however, we will remain out of touch with the emotions that help us select the best option for that situation.

Ideally, the sequence would go as follows:

1. Sensory experience
2. Emotions
3. Feelings (interpretion of the emotions)
4. Thoughts
5. Action

New information coming to us passes through the lower areas of the brain before reaching the neocortex. The lower areas of the brain, particularly the amygdala, work in a fraction of a second whereas the neocortex functions more slowly. Usually thought, however, is connected with an emotion. With high self-awareness we can detect the emotion that's connected to a thought.

There are some, however, who strive to go directly from experience to thought, bypassing emotions. They believe it is the enlightened approach to solving problems. In doing so, they may miss some important data that comes from their emotional brain. Emotions are data that can assist us in making wise decisions. People who lack self-awareness, however, will miss the important information that can be provided by the limbic (emotional) brain.

When corporate executives are asked how they make important decisions, their answer usually is as follows: "Well, I get as much data as is available to me at the time. I'll make sure the best research on the subject is at hand. I'll want to talk with my staff to get their perspective on the issue . . . and then I'll make a gut decision." The reason they get paid the big bucks is because their "gut decisions" are usually the best for the company. Gut decisions are "emotions" backed by a sound rationale. Pure reason or logic will not automatically point to the best decisions. It would be easy if it were that simple. Complex decisions need to involve our values and beliefs that reside in the emotional part of the brain, and these need to be combined with the best logical sequences being considered. Without self-awareness, the best combination of thoughts and emotions will not be possible.

In some instances, people go from experience to emotions and get stuck there. As a radical example, we can think of the thousands of people in prison today because of crimes of passion. "He made me mad, so I shot him." These individuals did not have access to the thoughts that would have them see the logical outcome if they merely acted on emotions.

A Story

John loved his new sports convertible, and driving it was the high point of his day. One afternoon, another driver ran a stop sign and smashed into John's car. John was furious and berated the other driver at the top of his voice. The language he used was humiliating and abusive. If a policeman were present, John could have been arrested for being totally out of control.

He was able to drive home, and when he arrived, his ten-year-old son's bicycle was lying in the driveway. John had to get out and move it so he could drive into the garage. When he came inside, his son was lying on the living room floor playing with Legos. John cuffed the boy hard on the back of the head and started berating *him*: "How many times do I have to tell you to park your bicycle beside the house? Put your toys away and go up to your room. No dinner for you tonight!" John then walked into the kitchen, where his wife, Ann, was arranging flowers. "Why isn't dinner on the table?" he shouted. "You know I get headaches when I'm hungry and can't eat. Must be nice to be able to stay home all day and do just what you please."

John was unaware that his foul mood from the car accident was pushing him to abuse his family. His lack of self-awareness sent him out of control, poisoning the atmosphere wherever he went.

With training and discipline John might develop enough self-awareness to change the way he behaved with others when angered. It is also possible he could continue to be oblivious to how his emotions dominated his words and behavior, likely resulting in an alienated relationship with his son, possibly a divorce, and few job enhancements. A dramatic incident in his life might be a wake-up call for him to learn greater self-awareness, or those same incidents could drive him into becoming an alcoholic. It remains a mystery why some people develop self-awareness and utilize that awareness to modulate their words and action and others do not. We are all likely aware of some people who appear condemned to simply remaining out of touch.

Out-of-control emotions always work against us. If we're angry, sarcastic, and belittling and don't even know it, three things are bound to follow. First—physiologically speaking—we are at risk of driving up our blood pressure or developing an ulcer. Second, lack of self-awareness, and therefore self-control, will lead us to violate our own values and standards. Third, we'll turn people off without understanding why. Obviously, what we don't recognize, we can't manage. In either case, we can see how self-awareness is so central to a successful career and a satisfying personal life.

The following two diagrams (tables 3.1 and 3.2) come from a PowerPoint presentation by the Hay Group in Boston, which uses them in training people to utilize their individual and 360 surveys in their recently revised Emotional and Social Competency Inventory.

Self-awareness also has a powerful connection to our leadership style. The Hay Group in Boston identified 436 managers who had taken the ESCI (Emotional and Social Competency Inventory) in 2009. When they divided the 436 managers into groups according to their self-awareness score, they discovered an astonishing relationship between a person's behavior and the climate of the whole organization. Of those leaders demonstrating high emotional self-awareness, 92 percent created the kind of positive climate within which their team was creative and high performing. Only 8 percent had a neutral impact, and none created a demotivating climate. In sharp contrast, 78 percent of leaders demonstrating low emotional self-awareness

TABLE 3.1. The Impact of Self-Awareness

		Self-Management	
		Yes	No
Self-Awareness	Yes	49%	51%
	No	4%	96%

Note: N= 427, p < .001
Source: Ruth Jacobs, PhD, Emotional Competence Inventory Accreditation Training, Philadelphia, PA (March 20–21, 2002).

Without self-awareness, a person has virtually no chance of demonstrating
self-management.

created negative climates, and only 22 percent of these leaders of teams had
a positive work climate. The implications of these finds can be instructive
when analyzing the emotional climate within a congregation.

Consider how a high level of self-awareness allows us to be a more
competent member of a work team. When a controversial issue is being
considered in a meeting, a self-aware individual is first aware of her own
emotional reaction to the conflict, both her anxiety and her rising anger,
which she will sit on for the moment, because surfacing it immediately
would not be helpful to the discussion. This person is also aware of the
tenseness of her body, and she might also notice fatigue from a lack of
sleep the night before. She may also be aware of the bond she experiences
with several members on the board. This self-awareness occurs at the same
time as she is monitoring the group process and where the argument is
taking the group. Since self-awareness is also essential for empathy, this
person can be keenly aware of how others in the group are reacting to the
process and even what they are not expressing. She might observe that a
few people feel intimidated by some members but not others. She might
also tune in to their sense of how the board chair is handling the meeting.
This combination of self-awareness and empathy allows this individual
to function with great competence in this meeting. She can avoid being
carried away by her emotions and exhibit behavior that makes her more
objective and hence more helpful in the meeting.

TABLE 3.2. The Impact of Self-Awareness

		Social Awareness	
		Yes	No
Self -Awareness	Yes	38%	62%
	No	17%	83%

Note: N= 427, p < .001
Source: Jacobs, 2002.

Without self-awareness, a person has an 83 percent chance of lacking social awareness.

If, however, we are aware of our behavior—if we understand why we are acting the way we are and how it's affecting others—we can change. With self-awareness, we are able to view our lives from a historical perspective as well as to consider how we would prefer to live our life. This stance enables us to discipline ourselves by delaying gratification to pursue the life we wish to create.

There is perhaps no psychological skill more fundamental than resisting impulses. It is the root of self-control. Self-awareness is key. We need to be aware of our drive for instant gratification and be able to view it with some objectivity. At the same time we can be aware of the goals we are able to achieve by delaying immediate gratification.

We all possess the potential for a greater level of self-awareness. The ability to observe our emotions, thoughts, and behavior dispassionately is more challenging for some than others, but either way the long-term rewards of greater self-awareness are huge.

In the process of growing in self-awareness, there are times when we recognize we are giving ourselves specific messages. In EQ parlance these messages are called "self-talk." These are messages we all give ourselves in the face of certain experiences. Some of these messages can be pretty negative. Without self-awareness, these messages will continue to play in the back of our minds, continually running us down. We end up having moods that we cannot understand. Some examples of self-talk: "You never

seem to manage details well. You're just an airhead." "You're stupid."
"You will never amount to anything." Likely, these are parental voices that
keep playing in our head without our being aware of them, rendering us
less competent than we might be if our self-talk were more positive. With
self-awareness, we at least have the opportunity to become conscious of
the negative self-talk and change these messages to more positive messages.
When we are emotionally healthy, we usually have self-talk that affirms
our worth and dignity. Affirmative self-talk can also make us more optimistic and positive.

Self-aware people also know what pushes their buttons and can guard
against negative reactions. We all have some neurotic patterns, and self-
aware people know when they are heading there and are able to choose
alternative behaviors. Someone who was abused as a child may move to a
fearful place any time another adult raises his or her voice. This emotion
may never ever go away, but it is possible through self-awareness to be
in touch with how scared we are while at the same time not act on that
fear. We can acknowledge the frightened child within us yet respond in a
mature, appropriate way.

Internal insecurity can also make us defensive when challenged or
given some strong, negative feedback. With heightened self-awareness,
however, we can monitor our defensiveness while at the same time we
learn to listen more attentively to what is being said. That, at least, allows
us the opportunity to learn more about ourselves and the person challenging us or giving us feedback—much better than going into meltdown.

There have been some disciplines that have been identified that can
assist us to increase self-awareness. Here are a few.

The Power of Meditation

Here is an oversimplified description of meditation. A person sits in a quiet
place with her eyes closed. While staying in the present (the here-and-
now moment), the subject pays attention to her thoughts and emotions.
As a warm-up exercise for this kind of meditation, an individual can count
how many thoughts appear in her mind in one minute. The count may
range from as few as five to as many as twenty thoughts. This exercise
demonstrates how wonderfully we are made. We can actually go to one
part of our brain and observe the activity of another part. This can be
called going to that place where we can be the watcher, the witness, the
observer. To develop self-awareness, we need to go to this place to observe

our thoughts, emotions, body sensations, and behavior. Meditation can be seen as another way of practicing such self-awareness.

In his research on the prefrontal lobes of the brain, University of Wisconsin neuroscientist Richard Davidson made an amazing discovery regarding meditation. The prefrontal lobes of the brain are a type of executive center of the mind. These lobes are the decision makers regarding whether a given situation requires moving to the fight/flight mode in a given situation or to a more calm response. When we are in our left prefrontal lobe, we are into sadness, feeling down, being depressed, feeling low, but when we are into our right prefrontal lobe, we are upbeat and happy, feeling positive about life. Most of us are a type of bell curve between these two lobes—that is, we spend about equal amounts of time in each lobe.

In a test group one morning, Davidson had a retired monk from a Buddhist monastery. To his surprise, this individual was way off the scale to the right (i.e., upbeat and happy). Davidson then began to wonder whether all meditators would score the same. He found the resources to conduct a similar test on other "supermeditators"—namely, people who had already meditated between thirty thousand to forty thousand hours in their life. With a few exceptions, he found that they, too, were way off the scale to the right. It appears that seasoned meditators are the most happy, upbeat people on the planet! Davidson subsequently proceeded to test people whom his team had put through an intensive forty-eight-hour meditation training course. Even though their training was slight, they also had moved farther to the right in their prefrontal lobes. As a result of some of this research, Davidson himself developed greater use of the practice of meditation in his own life.

Tibetan Buddhists believe that the essence of life is happiness. They believe that anyone can be happy if one makes meditation a priority in one's daily life. To quote the Dalai Lama in *The Essence of Happiness*, "You may be economically poor, not feeling the best physically, your marriage may be on the rocks, but if you have your mind you have all the essential tools you need to be happy." In his small book *The Pocket Dalai Lama*, he goes on to say, "The basic fact is that humanity survives through kindness, love and compassion. That human beings can develop these qualities is their real blessings."[3]

During their meditative time, Buddhist monks are taught not to indulge in specific negative feelings during practice. Buddhist teachers call these "destructive emotions." Daniel Goleman collaborated with the Dalai

Lama in a book titled *Destructive Emotions*. Two major destructive emotions to turn off are anger and fear. Our minds can get carried away by these two emotions. Although they may have some initial things to teach us, indulging these emotions will cause us to sink deeper and deeper into a negative hole. Realizing we are sinking into such a hole and putting a stop to it takes self-awareness. Other destructive emotions include sadness, disgust, craving, contempt, and delusion. When monks, in their meditation practice, notice they are going down any one of these destructive paths, they consciously turn away and open themselves to more neutral or positive emotions.[4] Without self-awareness, this would not be possible.

Human Relations Groups

Self-awareness and other skills in emotional intelligence are a major focus in basic human relations training groups. In the human relations training sponsored by the EQ-HR Center, people are placed in small groups of eight to twelve people with two training specialists—best when such a workshop lasts for five days, but significant learnings can occur in shorter time periods. In these small groups, trainers offer the group no leadership whatsoever. Silence reigns until someone takes the initiative to fill the vacuum. The norm in such small-group work is that participants are to stay in the here-and-now moment. Participants talking about their past is strongly discouraged, because when people talk about their past, other group members can do little for them. Instead, participants are encouraged to stay in the here and now and express the feelings going on inside of them at the moment.

Discussing what they are experiencing in the moment is a real challenge for people who are not very self-aware. Some are not used to talking about feelings. Usually, thoughts, rather than feelings, emerge first, and participants are challenged to move from their thoughts to their feelings. In this sharing of feelings in the "here and now," participants get to know each other very well. As the process continues, people can begin to offer feedback on the impact that other people's words and behaviors have on them. This is often called experiential learning. It is taking emotional intelligence beyond what can be learned in an academic format. In order to continue to participate in "here-and-now" time, participants need to continually be aware of internal thoughts and feelings, as these shift as group life evolves. Authenticity can be seen as our ability to share with the group what is really going on inside of us in the moment. For some, this may be the first time they are affirmed for being real in the moment and sharing what is going on internally.[5]

Keeping a Journal

Other people have found that the discipline of journaling has taught them much about self-awareness. This discipline is different from keeping a diary—that is, simply recording the events of the day. One may reflect on events, but the focus should be on the feelings experienced related to those events. The process of journaling helps the writer to identify feelings that were not accessible to the writer while an event was occurring. Sometimes people are surprised by what emerges when engaging in this type of self-reflection. As they continue in this discipline, people can learn how to be more self-aware in the moment.

Self-Awareness in the Life and Teaching of Jesus

The notion of self-awareness is absolutely fundamental in Jesus' teachings and in the Gospels. Though the term is a modern one, it points to one of the most essential qualities of the follower of Jesus.

The synoptic Gospels place the story of Jesus' temptation or testing in the wilderness (i.e., the Judean desert) at the beginning of Jesus' ministry. The point is not merely that Jesus' ministry begins at this time. The writers were asserting that testing was both the means by which Jesus prepared for his mission and the way he demonstrated his readiness for it. It was the indispensible prelude to the struggle that would follow against demons and opponents. Being tested, the Gospels imply, strengthened Jesus. Jesus' refusal to be lured by empty promises tells hearers a good deal about Jesus, the human one.

The desert, in biblical tradition, was a place of cleansing, of confrontation with oneself, free from all distractions, a lonely and demanding place of testing—and developing self-awareness. By placing the temptation story as the prelude to Jesus' ministry, the Gospels are saying that this confrontation with one's demons is the paradigmatic experience necessary for true discipleship. It is certainly no accident that Jesus is said to have withdrawn by himself to quiet places to pray—a kind of brief return to the desert and an example for his followers. The desert fathers and mothers were deeply aware of this, which is why they went into the desert and developed spiritual practices that involved a profound appropriation of the teachings of Jesus.[6]

The importance of testing is also shown by its prominence in the Lord's Prayer. In this prayer, we ask God not to put us to the test, but rather to deliver us from the evil one. We acknowledge how ill prepared we are to face temptation or testing. That is, we know ourselves that we are self-aware and that by ourselves are unable to survive real testing. A new translation of the Lord's Prayer appropriately uses the word "test" rather than "temptation," since the word "temptation" is so often trivialized—for example, when we say we are "tempted" by chocolate. Yet we also know that temptation will happen—not just trivial temptations but the kind that Jesus faced: temptations to disobedience, to self-glorification, to seeking the praise of others.

The *absence* of self-awareness has a specific name in the Gospels: hypocrisy. Jesus is portrayed as especially critical of hypocrites—those who would tell others how to live while they themselves failed to do those very things. Discipleship and hypocrisy are totally incompatible. Therefore, Jesus asked, "Why do you see the speck in your neighbor's eye, but do not notice the log in your own eye? Or how can you say to your neighbor, 'Let me take the speck out of your eye,' while the log is in your own eye?" (Matthew 7:3–4/Luke 6:41–42). These questions address two situations: ordinary human relationships (Matthew 7:3) and situations in which religious leaders claim to be guides to the blind (Matthew 7:4). Jesus asked rhetorically, "Can a blind person guide a blind person?" (Luke 6:39). Jesus recognized the importance of leaders who are self-aware and who subject themselves to rigorous self-examination.

The desert is a place free from worldly distraction, but this place can be found without going to the desert—namely, by abandoning the things to which one clings as essential to one's life. This is why Jesus tells his followers, "Sell your possessions, and give alms" (Luke 12:33). And then he provides a way by which one can come to deeper knowledge of oneself: "For where your treasure is, there your heart will be also" (Luke 12:34). Jesus was talking not only about money but about all those things we deem essential in our lives, all our passions and desires, all our "needs."

One of the most severe demands Jesus placed on his followers was to totally refrain from judging others (Matthew 7:1). Why was this so important? Not judging means that one is so acutely aware of his own deficiencies that he has no basis for judging others, and judging others means that one lacks awareness of these deficiencies. So it is no surprise that, in Matthew, the explicit demand to recognize the log in one's own eye before attempting to extract the speck in someone else's eye immediately follows the command not to judge (Matthew 7:3–5).

Lest self-awareness breed self-absorption, Jesus commanded humility as well as love of others. The link between self-awareness and regard for others is especially clear in the so-called Golden Rule. This rule, which Jesus was not the first to formulate, calls for self-awareness, especially in Jesus' version of it: "Do to others as you would have them do to you" (Luke 6:31/Matthew 7:12). To obey this mandate would require self-awareness, awareness of the feelings and reactions of others, humility, and empathy—in short, emotional intelligence.

The notion of self-awareness is a modern way of expressing an ancient concept, not unique to Jesus but emphasized by him with peculiar force. The Wisdom tradition in the books of Proverbs and Sirach addresses in detail the need for self-control, the need to not be impulsive but to react thoughtfully, the need to avoid letting anger seize control of us. In fact, "wisdom" in this tradition is not understood as knowledge of facts. It is a form of self-discipline, a way of living, and few really attain this wisdom. It must be gained through testing, through patience. Paul offered a nice summary of how wisdom is attained, though he does not use the word "wisdom": "Suffering produces endurance, and endurance produces character, and character produces hope" (Romans 5:3–4). He continues by showing that our relationship with the divine undergirds the whole process. Jesus stood within this Wisdom tradition, though also within the prophetic tradition.

Ancient Greek philosophy also focused on how one should live a virtuous life.[7] For example, self-knowledge played a special role for Socrates, who tried to live out the admonition inscribed at the shrine of Delphi: "Know thyself." He told the jurors at his trial that the unexamined life is not worth living. He himself claimed to know nothing and focused on helping others come to self-awareness.

Through the centuries, Christians, influenced in part by Greek philosophy, came up with a variety of lists of virtues, one of the best-known lists being the "cardinal virtues" of temperance, prudence, courage, and justice. These virtues describe a way of life that is characterized by self-reflection, restraint, care for others, humility, and also the courage to live by these virtues. Self-awareness, rather than being a foreign import or modern idea, is deeply rooted in Christian tradition and in Jesus' life and teachings. It is really the indispensible condition for true spiritual maturity.

The role of self-awareness will again become evident when we discuss Jesus' demands that we forgive without limit, that we love our enemies, that we count the cost of following him, that we love our neighbors as ourselves, and others of his radical demands. We will discuss forgiveness at greater length later. None of these can be enacted without genuine and honest self-awareness.

FOUR

Empathy and Jesus

For twenty-five years, Chuck Lewis, an ordained Evangelical Lutheran Church in America (ELCA) pastor, was the night minister in San Francisco's Tenderloin area as part of an ecumenical ministry supported by congregations in that city. At about 11:00 p.m., he would put on his clerical collar and begin walking the streets of the city. Volunteers would handle telephone calls that came in to a suicide prevention center. When a call came in from someone in trouble, they would call Chuck, and he would immediately go to be with the person. He was an empathic presence to this person as well as to many of the street people who lived in the Tenderloin. Chuck was able to do this for so many years because he could be fully present to people in pain or difficulty without personally taking on each person's pain or difficulty. He knew the difference between empathy and sympathy, and that made him effective in this calling. Over time, he became a trusted person on the streets of the city. Often, he would visit bars where bartenders kept him up to date on what was happening in their area and pointed out who needed special attention.

What Is Empathy?

Daniel Goleman observes, "In today's psychology, the word 'empathy' is used in three distinct senses: *knowing* another person's feelings, *feeling* what that person feels, and *responding* compassionately to another's distress. In short, I notice you, I feel with you, so I act to help you."[1] Chuck Lewis had all these qualities, plus one more: he wanted to be true to his ordination vows to be the living presence of Christ to the street people in San Francisco.

When Chuck encountered a street person or someone in a personal crisis, he was able to connect in some way with each individual. Another word for empathy is "attunement." We become attuned to what is transpiring within another person.

Empathy entails projecting oneself into another's situation without at the same time taking on that person's feelings. Being able to sense another person's internal state, including thoughts and feelings, is a gift. Some people have more empathy than others, but all of us can be trained to develop it. Those with great capacity for empathy usually gravitate toward professions where empathy is central, such as psychotherapy, congregational ministry, social work, or other helping professions. Yet all professions require some empathic skills. Without an ability to intuit what is going on inside another person, how can we possibly begin to relate to him or her? We need to have some idea of the emotional state of another person if we are to connect with that person.

Empathy builds on our capacity for self-awareness. It is difficult to be attuned to another person's inner reality if we have not been or rarely are in tune with our own.

Our capacity for empathy involves the use of mirror neurons in the brain. Their function, described in detail by neuroscientist Marco Iacoboni, is complex.[2] The brain contains about a hundred billion neurons, but only a few are mirror neurons. In the region of the neocortex where mirror neurons were first found, about 20 percent of the neurons are mirror neurons.[3] These neurons allow us to imitate the actions of others and thus to learn from them. You may have noticed that during conversation with a friend, he adopts the same posture as you, or vice versa. So, for example, you both might find yourselves resting your right cheekbone on one fist and later shifting posture almost simultaneously. Mirror neurons enable us to imitate others' behaviors. But also, according to Iacoboni, "mirror neurons let us understand the intentions of other people."[4] Thus, "mirror neurons show the deepest way we relate to and understand each other; they demonstrate that we are wired for empathy."[5] Advances in neuroscience have enabled us to understand the parts of the brain involved in empathy. Simon Baron-Cohen says, "There is a consensus in neuroscience that at least ten interconnected brain regions are involved in empathy (and more may await discovery)."[6] He identifies and succinctly describes these,[7] but for our purposes, these details are not essential. However, Baron-Cohen is especially interested in the fact that people do not have equal amounts of empathy. He has devised a bell curve of empathy, with a scale from zero to nine, based on his findings that most people possess a moderate ability to empathize, the numbers dwindling toward either extreme. He links the absence of empathy to disorders such as autism (a harmless form) and psychopathology (a dangerous form). The significance of the discovery that the brain is hardwired for empathy is that it opens up the possibility of finding ways to treat disorders linked to lack of empathy and ways to enhance empathy for those whose level of empathy is low.

People who lack the capacity for empathy can become abusers of others. Wife beaters, rapists, and child molesters would not do these horrific things if they had the capacity to empathize with others, to recognize their fear and pain. While not the only factor contributing to criminality, the lack of empathy is certainly a crucial element.[8] In fact, our capacity for *moral development* depends upon our capacity for empathic response to others. Deficits in empathy may significantly retard moral development. People in prison for violating other human beings are fortunate if they receive treatment in prison that enables them to empathize with others. When personnel supervising an inmate's progress in empathy finally observe that the inmate is able to identify with the feelings of the person he or she abused, they know that rehabilitation is finally working. Those who learn this skill have a better chance of being restored to society.

Key to intuiting another's emotions is an ability to read nonverbal communication: tone of voice, gesture, facial expressions, irritation in the quickness of a gesture, and the like.[9] Goleman cites a test with 1,001 children and notes, "Those who showed an aptitude for reading feelings nonverbally were among the most popular in their schools, the most emotionally healthy."[10] Goleman also recalls the rule of thumb used in communication research that 90 percent or more of an emotional message is nonverbal.[11]

Paul Ekman and Wallace Friesen discovered over a period of years that many facial expressions are universal.[12] The hundred-plus muscles in the face will move in predictable patterns when specific emotions are experienced. Ekman has devised a way of teaching people who need to read emotions (e.g., TSA officials, police officers, and the like) how to do this instinctively. In a fraction of a second, he will flash before an individual any of seven expressions: sadness, anger, fear, surprise, disgust, contempt, or happiness. At first, people can get only about 50 percent of them correct, because they are trying to figure out these expressions cognitively. This skill belongs to the low road, the amygdala, rather than the high road of the neocortex. When people are given feedback about when they guessed right and when they were wrong, they can develop the capacity to get 80 to 90 percent of the expressions right. Developing this skill increases our capacity for empathy.[13]

A colleague of Roy's, G. Brent Darnell, is a human relations/emotional intelligence freelance consultant to the construction industry. He has a track record of teaching empathy to construction workers, especially those in the role of foreman. This is detailed in his book *The People-Profit Connection*.[14] Brent goes into construction companies stating that he will increase the profits of their company if they are willing to contract his services teaching EQ to their workers. He continues to make a fine living working such contracts because his results continue to impress corporate executives.

He begins by administering the EQ-i MHS survey to company foremen. The average score overall for assertiveness is 100. The majority of foremen tested score 120 or higher in assertiveness but mostly below 80 on empathy. When the workers first look at their results, they laugh at their low scores in empathy. They think it is funny. "Ha-ha, I got 70 on empathy. What did you get?" "Yeah, I got only 66 on mine." Who wants to work for a foreman who scores 120 on assertiveness and under 70 on empathy? For example, some worker may show up late because his wife was ill and he was up all night with her at the emergency ward of a hospital. A typical response to this news by a foreman might be "I don't give a damn that you stayed up all night with your wife in the hospital. Get your ass up on the roof, and start putting on shingles." Most construction foremen believe you need to be tough if you are to get your money's worth out of workers. Brent tries to show these foremen that if they showed even a little bit of empathy for their workers, they wouldn't have so much internal conflict and job turnover. After getting into their heads that a little more empathy would do the company a whole lot of good, Brent sends these people home to practice empathy with their wives. They are supposed to say, "Honey, tell me about your day," and then really listen. In the past, these men were not good listeners. When their wives would share a problem they encountered during the day, the first response of the male spouse would be to try to fix it for his wife. "Why didn't you try this—or try that?" These males would then get angry because their wives didn't take well to their advice. But Brent coaches them not to go that route. When their wives share a problem, they are supposed to try to be empathic and express that empathy by saying, "Gee, honey, you must have been feeling _____ when that happened." With practice, some of these husbands get to be pretty good at being empathetic with their spouses. Some come back to Brent after a few weeks of this, saying, "You know, this stuff is really great. My love life hasn't been this good in years."

The effect on the construction company is even more dramatic. Absenteeism falls dramatically, sick days decline, there is greatly reduced job turnover, company morale rises dramatically, and profits hit all-time highs.

When we truly feel understood by another person, the nature of our relationship with the person changes dramatically for the better. How deeply we crave to be understood at a deep level! When we truly feel understood, we will likely be willing to "break a leg" to do what's needed for that person. Theologian Martin Buber called such authentic connections between people "I-Thou" relationships, in contrast to "I-it" relationships that treat others as objects. Treating a person as though that person were an "it" is seeing him or her only as someone I might be able to use for my self-interest. When in an "I-Thou" relationship, however, two people become the whole world to each other. To quote Goleman, "All communication requires that what matters for the sender also matters for the receiver. By sharing thoughts as well as feelings, two brains deploy a shorthand that gets both people on the same page immediately, without having to waste time or words explaining more pointedly what matters are at hand."[15]

It can be exhilarating when two people are in sync with each other at this deep level. These may be short-term experiences as we may quickly revert back to pursuing our own interests, but these moments are remembered and are sought after again and again. At the core of these experiences is our capacity for empathy.

In some sense, empathy is projecting oneself into another's situation without at the same time taking on that person's feelings. A statement such as "Gosh, you seem really down on yourself. Is that because of what just happened?" can be a very empathic response to someone who is struggling with his own feelings. If the observation is on target, the person hearing it will certainly feel understood. When an attempt at empathy does not connect with the other person, we may be able to pick up on the fact that we were off target with our response and then, possibly, have another chance at empathy if the conversation continues. We will not be on target all the time. What matters most is our motivation to become better at this trait. Effectiveness in both our personal and professional lives depends upon this.

In the chapter on the emotionally intelligent congregation, we talk about having more church members, in addition to the pastoral staff, offering pastoral care to other members. The key to this is identifying lay-persons skilled in empathy for this ministry.

What Empathy Is Not

a) We often confuse empathy and agreement, thinking that if we are empathizing with someone it means that we are conceding that that person is right. The opposite of agreement is disagreement, and the opposite of empathy is apathy. It is possible to listen to someone in an empathetic way, and then let him or her know that we see things differently.

b) We may confuse empathy with sympathy. Empathy keeps the subject of the conversation on the other person. Sympathy is taking on the emotional load of another. It shifts from "you" to "I." "I am deeply moved by your setback." The speaker is attempting to state his or her reactions, thoughts, or emotions. Sympathy may be offered, but only after empathy is first expressed. Consider a doctor serving in the emergency ward of a hospital. This doctor would burn out quickly if he or she took on the pain of everyone coming through the door. Instead, the doctor can be totally present, in the moment, with a wounded or sick person and not be burdened by that person's pain as he or she moves on to serve another. The same is true of clergy who deal with a funeral of a beloved member at 11:00 in the morning and then preside at the wedding of other friends at 2:00 that afternoon. An empathic pastor can be truly present with the grief of those attending the funeral and then be equally present with the joy of friends who just got married. This pastor can be fully present with congregants at these two congregational events, and then be fully present with his son who is playing a championship soccer game at school, and be fully present with his spouse who has just come home after a trying day at her job. Both church and family function well because of the empathic skills of this self-aware pastor who does not personally take on the burdens of those to whom he relates.

c) We assume we are being empathic when we tell another about a similar experience we have had personally. Once again, we are shifting the focus of the conversation from this other person to ourselves.

d) We assume that empathy is simply being civil to others, displaying basic manners and courtesy, or just generally being nice to everyone. Nice is superficial, easy, and the minimum we can offer. Empathy needs to go much deeper.

e) Empathy is more than taking an intellectual stance on someone's personal dilemma. Giving someone an academic understanding of what this person is experiencing will likely come across as being cold and distant.

f) By empathizing with someone, we are not agreeing to take on the other person's issues nor are we obligated to try to fix them. We do not need to go beyond simply understanding what the other person is facing at the moment. The other person may even resent our presuming to take responsibility for his or her life.

Impediments to Empathy

a) We are hardwired to judge everything in order to maintain our physical and psychological safety. Judging another person (while listening) keeps us from connecting with them.

b) Empathy is nearly impossible if we are in the grip of stress. When our amygdala has hijacked our brain, we will have great difficulty empathizing with someone else. Because empathy is so crucial to spiritual maturity, we believe that the cultivation of empathy needs to be a central task of congregations. Among other things, this means seeking to promote understanding of marginalized and feared groups, challenging congregants to cast out fear, and providing accurate information during times when fear begins to take over. Fear is a great enemy of empathy. When we are scared, it is really difficult to express empathy with others, particularly with the persons who appear to threaten us.

c) Fear can be addressed by challenging the stereotypes of blacks, Jews, Arabs, Palestinians, welfare moms, Native Americans, assertive women, obese people, and, especially these days, Muslims. Philosopher Martha Nussbaum, alarmed by the rise of Islamophobia in the United States, has written a fine book on the fear of religious and cultural difference, *The New Religious Intolerance: Overcoming the Politics of Fear in an Anxious Age*.[16] The book is wide ranging, not confined to Islamophobia, and makes use of the neuroscience of fear. Congregations that address any of the fears of persons mentioned above are opening ways for its members to move toward greater empathy with the plight of others.

d) In addition to stress, if we don't feel worthy in a situation, we are more likely to expend emotional energy on our own personal issues than to "heart-listening" to others. Having high self-regard enables our capacity for empathy but does not ensure it.

e) In the workplace, understanding the duties and demands being placed on fellow staff members creates cohesive functioning. Understanding others' points of view will help make them team players. It is a real challenge trying to develop an effective working team when the capacity for empathy is low among team members.

Empathy is often practiced in EQ-HR workshops. Individuals are put in small groups of four to six people. One person is to share a real-life incident, one that has some emotional complexity, and the other group members take a turn empathizing with that individual, both tracking exactly what the person said and identifying the emotion that the person was going through at each stage of the story.[17] This exercise often reveals that some individuals are not very good at empathizing with others. We may think we are being empathic with our responses, but in life we rarely get any feedback as to when we are off target with our remarks; therefore, we lack opportunities to learn how to do it better.

The Use of Empathy in Group Process

Within a task group such as a congregational committee, it is important to differentiate between task and process. When such a group takes on an issue, such as addressing a leak in the church roof, and searches for some consensus from the group, the content of that discussion is considered its task. Process is the way the group functions in arriving at such a decision. People with process skills rely on their capacity for both self-awareness and empathy to pick up on what is happening within the group.

When, for example, the tone of a meeting begins to become adversarial, a person with good process skills will first become aware of negative feelings within herself. She also has the capacity to pick up negative feelings others are having about the meeting. For the meeting to stop heading in the negative direction, someone needs to have the courage to make a process intervention. A committee member might say, "Can we stop our discussion for a minute and talk about how we're going about our task? I sense from the way we're responding to one another that the meeting is becoming quite negative. In addition, we really don't seem to be listening to one another."

Some people in that same meeting might dismiss such a process intervention with comments such as "There you go again, bringing up that touchy feely stuff again. Can't we just proceed with the meeting and let the chips fall where they may? Are we all that fragile in this meeting?" On the other hand, someone might say, "Yes, I haven't been feeling good about our process. Thanks for mentioning this to us," moving the meeting in a more positive direction. The group could then decide to go about its decision making in a different way. If people don't feel good about the way a decision was made, they will have a hard time getting motivated to implement it. This is why a healthy, supportive process is required to reach high-quality decisions that people are motivated to implement.

Congregations with empathic group facilitators chairing meetings will find that the emotional tone of the congregation continually moves in a positive, upbeat direction. Here is where a congregation is able to teach its active members better, emotionally intelligent ways of interacting with one another. When meetings are conducted with positive process interventions, other group members learn how to monitor and contribute to group life. These may be members who did not experience an emotionally intelligent family life growing up, but they can learn to develop better self-awareness and empathy skills by simply being members of such a congregation. These are some long-term growth experiences that teach its members how to live more emotionally intelligent lives in other contexts of their life. We believe Jesus taught his disciples both self-awareness and empathy by the way their life together was managed.

Jesus and Empathy

Can we learn anything from Jesus about empathy and its role in his ministry? The word "empathy" is not used in the Gospels; in fact, it is a modern word.[18] However, the term "to have* compassion" (*splagchnizomai*), which refers to a sensation in the innards, regarded as the seat of emotions, is used many times in the Gospels and, as an emotional response to the plight of another, can probably be equated with what we now call empathy.[19] This word was not used metaphorically for "compassion" or "pity"

_____
*The term is a verb, not a noun.

in Greek literature, but it is found in late Jewish literature (in Greek) to designate *specifically divine compassion*. The word occurs only in the synoptic Gospels in the New Testament and is used primarily of Jesus.[20] The way this term is used in the Gospels, therefore, suggests that Jesus was understood as the vehicle of divine compassion. The Gospels portray Jesus as one in whom the compassionate heart of God came to expression.

While Jesus' compassion seems especially close to what we call empathy, the word "mercy" also presumes empathy on the part of the one who shows mercy. Jesus said, "Blessed are those who show mercy. They will be shown mercy [by God]" (Matthew 5:7). This translation from the New International Reader's Version of the Bible (as opposed to the traditional "blessed are the merciful") captures the nature of mercy as *acts* that arise out of compassion; the merciful do not merely feel kindly toward the unfortunate. When those afflicted with a disease cry out, "Have mercy," they are not pleading to be regarded with kindness; they want help.[21] In the Old Testament, God is portrayed as merciful because God actually helps God's people, which reflects God's tender care and love.

In the Sermon on the Mount, acts of mercy are to be done without anyone noticing, without calling attention to one's act (Matthew 6:1–4). They are to be "unrecognizable as good deeds and thus done in imitation of the invisibility of God."[22] Acts of mercy should flow un-self-consciously, without the left hand knowing what the right hand is doing (Matthew 6:3). This means that empathy has to be ingrained, second nature, and automatic; it imitates the graciousness of God.

We have argued in chapter 2 that Jesus' healings required profound empathy with those who were ill. This empathy would have been readily detected or sensed by the ill whom he encountered, triggering a deep emotional resonance in the ill persons. The Gospels call this resonance "faith," and this faith or trust in Jesus was apparently what made the healing possible. Empathy can be healing.

The healings of marginalized persons—women, especially deeply disturbed women like Mary Magdalene (Luke 8:2), persons deemed religiously unclean, crazed people like the Gadarene (or Gerasene) demoniac (Mark 5:1–20)—tell us that Jesus had no fear of such people. He had cast out fear. His contagious empathy must have also enabled fearful, ostracized persons to overcome their own fears of approaching him. Fear of the marginalized, or of associating with them, would have made empathy impossible.

In Matthew 5:23–24, Jesus says, "So when you are offering your gift at the altar, if you remember that your brother or sister has something against you, leave your gift there before the altar and go; first be reconciled to your brother or sister" (cf. Mark 11:25). To be conscious of how one's actions might have aroused anger or offense in others would require empathy. Reconciliation with others is to take priority over religious acts, which means that empathy must be a basic characteristic of those who love and honor God. In fact, the text seems to assume that religious acts—worship—in some way derive their meaning from, and require, reconciliation with others. Without that, they are empty gestures.

Jesus' empathic relationships with people were grounded in an understanding of God as gracious, merciful, indiscriminately showering blessings on rich and poor, righteous and unrighteous. A different understanding of God, such as a God who is cold, distant, or vindictive, would not be likely to evoke empathy. If congregations wish to cultivate empathy among members, they may wish to consider what images of God are being presented in their liturgy, art, sermons, and educational programs. Moreover, do they (like the parable of the Good Samaritan) work to reduce fear of others, especially those who are marginalized?

Conclusion

At the beginning of this chapter, we noted that empathy can include knowing another person's feelings, feeling what that person feels, and responding compassionately. We have the capacity for empathy because our brains evolved to create and maintain relationships with others, which are necessary for human flourishing, not to mention safety, productivity, and enjoyment. When the capacity for empathy is lacking or underdeveloped, the person is likely to have retarded moral development and/or poor relational skills and may even be a danger to others. Criminals are likely to be among those with underdeveloped empathic capacity.

To be empathic requires a set of skills including the ability to read tone of voice, gesture, facial expression, and body language. These skills are needed because most of the emotional content in relationships is nonverbal. Pastors as well as laypersons lacking these skills are not likely to function effectively in relationships. Fortunately, empathy can be learned or developed more fully. Congregations and pastors would be wise to consider ways in which this might be done.

We have set forth Jesus as an exemplar of the capacity for empathy. But we also saw some ways in which his practice and teaching of empathy go beyond conventional emotional intelligence treatments of empathy. First, Jesus' empathy was rooted in his view of God as kind, merciful, and indiscriminately gracious to all. Second, Jesus insisted that his followers put their empathic skills into practice through acts of mercy for others and through giving priority to reconciliation with others. Finally, Jesus showed that empathy is healing; his healing ministry, we argued, was founded on creating empathic relationships with hurting people.

FIVE

Assertiveness and Jesus

Assertiveness is an acquired skill that involves being clear about where one is emotionally, one's needs and wants, and one's objections to certain things such as boundaries and limitations, while at the same time being concerned about the impact one's behavior has on others. Assertive people are not shy about expressing their point of view but do so without being aggressive or abusive. Being assertive is simply stating clearly who we are and what our perspective is. This may include how I will and will not allow others to treat me.

Interest in assertiveness arose in part out of the women's movement in the 1970s. Women were no longer willing to remain passive in the face of male domination. They learned to be more assertive, especially in the workplace, where they fought for equal pay for equal work. Men, who were used to women being passive, claimed that assertive women were being too aggressive and had all kinds of nasty names for them. During the civil rights struggle, African Americans faced the same challenge—to assert their needs and wants without becoming aggressive. Some African Americans did turn to violence, but leaders such as Martin Luther King Jr. preached assertiveness without violence. All of us, both men and women, can learn much by being appropriately assertive. Passive men are often called milquetoasts and are not respected, while overly aggressive males are often called "macho" or bulldogs and are avoided by many.

51

This has been the challenge of any minority group in our culture when it is no longer willing to remain passive and tolerate the abuse of the majority culture. Without being assertive, they will remain a disadvantaged minority. Minority persons often find that the majority culture can become quite aggressive in trying to keep them in their places. Those in power in our country always have law enforcement agencies there to protect their rights and property. Any minority pressing for equal rights will always, at least initially, have to put up with the aggressive tactics of those in power, which is backed up by the police.

We practice assertiveness because we seek to avoid certain negative behaviors. On one side is passive behavior—acting like a doormat, allowing others to trample over us any time they please. Passive people may simply be out of touch with what they need and want. It is hard to go after what you want when that remains unclear to you. Some passive people do know what they think and feel but are afraid to express it openly. When asked what they want or need, they obfuscate and express themselves so unclearly that they rarely get what they really want or need. Many just don't feel it is right to be so blatant about what they want. Quite possibly, as children, they were previously punished for being clear about their needs and wants.

On the other side is aggression—imposing our will on others without any concern for the impact this will have on them. Micromanaging others is a form of aggressive behavior. The micromanager does not recognize or embrace the creativity of others, is unable to delegate, cannot work as a team member, and does not trust others to do their jobs—a mistrust that is acutely experienced by others. Passive aggression seems passive but actually conceals aggressive intentions. It can include pouting, manipulation, whining, or simply remaining silent and passive but internally knowing that one will not do what is demanded while pretending to agree in the moment. It is like a worker who is berated by his boss for working slowly, but the worker continues to lumber along, getting even less accomplished. It can be as toxic to a group as aggressive behavior.

This is where aggressive people dig themselves into a different kind of hole than passive people. Their consistent demands turn others off, and people are not motivated to work with or for them. When supervisors consistently abuse the people who work under them, their workers will learn to do only as much as is demanded. Workers with aggressive bosses may live in fear that they will lose their jobs if they object to their boss's behavior. They may even put in a great deal of extra hours just to keep their jobs. When they find alternative work, however, they leave. High turnover of personnel is common in companies that tolerate or even support supervisors who show few signs of emotional intelligence.

This is where increased self-awareness is a necessary underpinning of assertive behavior. First of all, we need to be clear internally about what we need and want. We also need to be aware of how scary it will be to state those needs and wants clearly, especially with people we know who will be thrown off balance by such clarity on our part. Assertiveness needs to be combined with the skill of empathy, which keeps us in touch with how stating our needs and wants will affect others. Empathy also puts us in touch with how we will need to state things in order to be heard by another. For some people, you need to hit them with the proverbial two-by-four in order to get their attention to the new behavior we need from them. With others, just the hint that we need something more or less from them makes them defensive.

Once we have engaged someone with our assertive words, we will need to remain both self-aware and empathic as we engage that person in dialogue about our desires. When we receive a strong negative response from someone or some group, we can become frightened and easily revert to passive behavior, trying to minimize the importance of what we are asking. On the other hand, we may receive a reaction from others that simply discounts what we are asking, and we will need to assert ourselves even more strongly of the importance of what we are asking of them while at the same time remaining concerned about others' feelings.

How to Be Properly Assertive

Assertive people are clear about what they need and want, but they also work hard to understand the needs and wants of others. When their needs and wants clash with the needs and wants of others, they are open to negotiate with them, exploring ways in which this can be a "win-win" for everyone.

There are usually four steps involved in managing a crisis situation while being open as well as assertive. We will use as an example of these four steps a situation in a multiple-staff congregation.

1. First, manage your own emotions while you inform the other that you're clearly aware of his or her situation regarding the matter about which you're going to assert yourself. Senior pastor Michael walks

in the office of his associate pastor Julie to relay a troubling situation that has just surfaced. "Julie, I know your husband Jake and you had planned to take your kids to the ocean this weekend. You have looked forward to this for several weeks."

2. Next, inform the other about your general situation regarding your request. "As you know, I will be tied up all day Saturday with a retreat with all our church officers. That retreat has been postponed twice already, and it's now or never. I've just been informed that Norm Nelson, who is both a friend and a pillar of this church, has unexpectedly died. The funeral has been set for 2:00 p.m. Saturday, as this is the only time his extended family in Michigan is able to attend."

3. Third, let the other know specifically what you'd like from him or her. "Julie, I need you to postpone that weekend with your family. At this late date, you are the only one who can lead portions of that retreat. I can be there for part of the time but not for a major portion of the event. I know you have the skills that are needed at that workshop."

4. Express appreciation and any reward as a result of this extra effort, ending up with a confirmation of acceptance. "In appreciation, I will go to bat for you so that you can have the entire Labor Day weekend at the shore with your family. I will also see to it that you have some extra time with your family over Christmas. I will mention the sacrifice you are making here at your annual review that's coming up this fall. May I count on you for that Saturday retreat?"

It's hard to say no to emotionally intelligent, assertive leaders. They have the ability to get important things done while maintaining a positive relationship with their workers.

Rabbi Edwin Friedman, who creatively appropriated and developed the family systems theory of Murray Bowen, developed an approach to leadership that has been widely used by church leaders, and that incorporates a sophisticated understanding of assertive leadership. For example, his posthumously published *A Failure of Nerve: Leadership in the Age of the Quick Fix* is a call to leaders to lead.[1]

When Assertiveness Becomes an Issue

We suspect that the perceived shortcomings of congregational leaders, both lay and ordained, may often revolve around chronically low levels of assertiveness or chronically high levels of assertiveness. High levels of assertiveness can bring instrumental rewards and short-term goal achievement but can be costly when relationships fray or fail to take root. By contrast, low levels of assertiveness can bring social benefits but can undermine goal achievement.[2] When the appropriate level of assertiveness is perceived, it basically disappears from view. Only too low or too high levels of assertiveness receive attention.

This suggests the importance of assertiveness in how congregational leaders are perceived. A pastor may be perceived as being a weak leader in one congregation but be viewed as being far too assertive in another. The first congregation may have had a history of strong, assertive pastoral leaders while the second congregation may have had a history of low-key pastors. Call or search committees would do well if they reviewed their history of pastoral leadership over time and try to call a new pastor who matches that history. It can be a costly mistake to try to call the next pastor to remedy the deficit of the former one.

Was Jesus Assertive?

If we are asked to characterize Jesus, most of us probably would not immediately think of the term "assertive." In the Gospels, Jesus is never called "assertive," and we are not aware of Greek words that capture what we mean by "assertive."[3] We are left to consider the way Jesus is portrayed and to ask whether "assertive" would be an appropriate word to describe Jesus. By assertive, we mean having the self-confidence to put oneself forward, to be clear about one's wishes and needs, but without being aggressive. "Speaking the truth in love" (Ephesians 4:15) might be a good, brief description of assertiveness. Given that definition, does "assertive" describe Jesus?

The Gospels often speak of Jesus' "authority" (*exousia*), but that is the capacity and authorization to do something (e.g., cast out demons), with the implication that this authorization is uncommon and special. There is a somewhat similar word—power (*dynamis*)—but this is a more general capacity to do something, without the implication of special authorization. But neither term, by itself, implies assertiveness, though to *claim* such authority and to act upon it would certainly seem to be assertive. Jesus claimed to be authorized (by God, we assume) to forgive sins, to cast out demons, to teach in new and challenging ways.

There is a whole literary subgenre in the Gospels in which assertiveness seems clearly to be a factor—namely, "controversy dialogues," where

Jesus engages in spirited debates with opponents and bests them. Usually, Jesus is found doing something (e.g., harvesting or healing on the Sabbath, having disciples who eat with unwashed hands) for which opponents attack Jesus, who then responds with a defense of the activity or confounds his opponents with counterquestions. In these controversy dialogues, Jesus certainly comes off as assertive but not really as aggressive. However, Jesus' accusations against the Pharisees (e.g., Matthew 23) are not merely assertive; they are aggressive, relentless, and pitiless. It would be hard to defend these tirades as emotionally intelligent, even if they reflect less of Jesus himself than of the rough debates between the early church and their Jewish coreligionists, later attributed to Jesus.[4]

Jesus is not the only one who is portrayed as assertive. Parents of ill children are assertive in seeking Jesus' healing. The Syrophoenician or Canaanite woman who sought help for her daughter was certainly assertive, and Jesus' initial rude response quickly gave way to admiration of her retort (Mark 7:24–30) and to healing the daughter.

Assertiveness is sometimes said to entail recognizing one's own personal "boundaries," what one is willing to allow and what one will not allow. Here is an example where Jesus assertively maintains his boundaries:

> At that very hour some Pharisees came and said to him, "Get away from here, for Herod [Antipas] wants to kill you." He said to them, "Go and tell that fox for me, 'Listen, I am casting out demons and performing cures today and tomorrow, and on the third day I finish my work. Yet today, tomorrow, and the next day I must be on my way.'" (Luke 13:31–33)

Jesus' "cleansing" of the temple is often cited as an example of Jesus' anger (which the text does not mention), but it certainly seems like an assertive act (Mark 11:15–18).

In sum, yes, Jesus is portrayed as assertive. But can we say that this was an exemplary characteristic of Jesus that we should emulate? Does Jesus teach us something about assertiveness that we might not learn elsewhere? Both questions should probably be answered in the negative. Yet had Jesus not been assertive, he would not have claimed the authority he said he had, nor would he have dared to heal the sick, summon followers, preach, and teach.

SIX

Optimism and Jesus

Optimism is the ability and willingness to see the positive side in life. People who are optimistic tend to expect good things to happen to them on most days. Even when facing adversity, optimists maintain a positive attitude. Optimists assume a measure of hope in their approach to the challenges before them and are able to roll with the punches. When they experience a setback, they do not view it as a long-term defeat but as something temporary that can be managed over time. They tend to believe that the only failure is the failure to learn. They expect to learn from small defeats, and such learning will make them better able to handle future challenges. They also tend to see more opportunities than barriers or threats in the future. Optimists also look positively upon others and expect the best from them.

Optimism is considered a major trait of emotional intelligence. The scholars behind the development of the two major EQ surveys in the country think that optimism is necessary for personal health and wholeness.[1] Optimistic people motivate themselves to attain important goals in life. As with all EQ traits, the capacity for optimism can be enhanced. We all have the capacity to choose the emotions that will dominate our lives, and healthy people choose to experience positive and optimistic feelings about their future. As with all EQ traits, the capacity for optimism can be enhanced.

Psychologist Martin Seligman has discovered three major attitudes that distinguish optimists from pessimists: First, optimists view downturns in their lives as temporary blips on the screen. They believe the bad times won't last forever, that the situation will turn around, and that troubles and difficulties are merely delayed success rather than outright defeat. Second, they tend to view misfortune as situational and specific, not another manifestation of long-standing and inescapable doom. Third, optimists don't immediately shoulder all the blame. They are open to accepting their part in what went wrong but also to considering other external causes of failure.[2] In contrast, pessimists see failure or setback as permanent, pervasive, and personal. They see any lapse as yet another example of how they screw up every time. Pessimists conclude that things fail because of their own incompetence and ineffectiveness. Others feel like they are victims—that someone (or the universe) is out to do them in. Much of this may be an overall pessimistic view of life, with the expectation of being victimized in some way.

In *The Emotional Life of Your Brain*, Richard Davidson uses the term "outlook" as a way of viewing a continuum between optimism and pessimism.[3] He warns against adopting an excessively positive outlook, as it might impair our ability to learn from our mistakes. It could also move us too quickly to seek immediate gratification rather than benefiting from delayed gratification by holding out for a better outcome in the long run. At the same time, Davidson comments that life can be miserable for those who have a pessimistic outlook. On a ten-point scale, with one being at the extreme end of pessimism and ten on the extreme end of optimism, a healthy outlook score would range between seven and nine. Our challenge is to mainly expect positive things to happen to us while at the same time remaining grounded in the realities of some setbacks. Davidson's research indicates that we are all naturally optimistic, so maintaining an appropriate level of optimism should not be a huge task. His research also means that pessimism is unnatural, so if we find ourselves in a bad mood most of the time, we need to learn why we are that way.

Greater self-awareness is central to getting us out of a depressed state of affairs. When it is lacking, everyone around us senses that we are in a bad mood, but we remain oblivious to it ourselves. Self-awareness also makes it possible for us to track a negative disposition back to whatever triggered it. At times, that may be all we have to do to get us to a more positive place, when we discover that what created a negative mood was not that important. It may be as small as a clerk making a cutting remark when we picked up our coffee at a shop. Then again, what set us off may be more substantive, like our twelve-year-old telling us as she was leaving to catch a bus and we were leaving on an extended business trip that we always put our work ahead of her. That remark may need some careful thought and reflection rather than dismissing it and going on our happy way. We can also seek out professional help if we can't seem to shake off such a negative mood in a short time. Possibly just being with a good friend may do the same for us.

Neuroscientist Elaine Fox claims in her book *Rainy Brain, Sunny Brain* that optimism is not the same as "positive thinking." She explains optimism this way:

> Our sunny brain circuits help us to stay focused on the things that bring us rewards, and this keeps us engaged in important tasks. Optimism is about more than feeling good; it's about being engaged with a meaningful life, developing resilience, and feeling in control. Optimistic realists, whom we consider to be the true optimists, don't believe that good things will come if they simply think happy thoughts. Instead, they believe at a very deep level that they have some control over their own destinies.[4]

Fox locates optimism in the pleasure center of the brain, the nucleus accumbens, which she describes as an "ancient structure that sits underneath the cortex, right at the front of the brain."[5] Two neurotransmitters, dopamine and the opioids, are the main sources of optimism.[6] She says, "It's the opioids that paint the pleasure gloss on our experiences, while dopamine keeps us coming back for more."[7] Both optimists and pessimists can sense pleasure; the difference is that in optimists, this sense of pleasure is sustained much longer. In addition, the nucleus accumbens sends signals to the prefrontal cortex, which inhibits overreaction to pleasure, helping us focus on long-term, not just immediate, pleasure. The result is a realistic optimist.

To better understand optimism, it is useful to consider what Fox calls the pessimistic or "rainy brain." Three structures are key: the thalamus (which is our more primitive brain mainly controlling bodily function), the amygdala, and the insula. Basically, the amygdala is extremely sensitive to threats, and the insula translates the fear signals from the amygdala into what we call "fear," which triggers the thalamus to stimulate a fear-related bodily response.[8] The "emergency brain" (mainly, the amygdala) has been trained over centuries of evolution not only to detect danger but also to seize control of the body and provoke flight-or-fight responses. The prefrontal cortex can judge whether there really is danger and, if so, how to respond to it. Regularly giving in to fear actually enhances the emergency brain's circuitry, thus making one more pessimistic. By contrast, optimism can become a sort of habit of the brain. The more the pathways linking different parts of the brain related to pleasure are used, the more they function like a stream that carves out a channel through the sand, enabling a sustained optimistic or "sunny brain." But continually triggering a fearful response to one's environment can lead to the development of gloomy thoughts, which can then escalate into enduring anxiety disorders.[9] In other words, we can train ourselves to become pessimists by focusing on fears and threats. Both optimism and pessimism can become habits. By the way we respond to the world around us, we can make ourselves pessimists or optimists.

Optimism, however, is not the absence of testing reality, and reality testing is considered an EQ trait. We are not advocating adopting a Pollyanna view of life. In the absence of reality testing there is a false optimism that can set a person up for some real setbacks. When those setbacks begin to occur more often, it can turn a positive view of life into a negative one. True optimism is a comprehensive and hopeful but realistic approach to daily living.

Appreciative Inquiry: A New Approach to Organizational Consultations

Within the past ten years an approach to consulting with corporations or other organizations called "appreciative inquiry" has emerged. In the past, consultants would begin an intervention by asking questions they hoped would explain why things were not working as well as desired. They would then try to fix what was wrong with the organization. Appreciative inquiry does just the opposite. It works first to surface all the positive things that are happening in a congregation or community. This reminds the *group* of all the great things it is currently doing. It is from this place of confidence that challenges can be addressed. It's a more optimistic way of dealing with problems.

Training for Optimism

Neuroscientists would characterize most of what we have said above as "mental training," or "brain training." We are exercising those parts of the brain that deal with positive emotions. In the chapter on self-aware-ness, we mentioned that Buddhist monks with between thirty thousand and forty thousand hours of meditation under their belts are some of the most optimistic people on the planet. In their meditation training they are instructed to avoid thoughts that lead to what they call "destructive emo-tions." Meditation can be considered a type of "brain training." Training in "appreciative inquiry" could be considered the same.

Working with affirmations can also be viewed as brain training. The basic theory behind affirmations is that we are giving our unconscious mind a direct message about how we would prefer to experience life. The theory claims that our unconscious mind is our friend and wants to do whatever it takes to make life better for us. Unfortunately, some of us rarely give our unconscious mind a direct message. We may think of all the good things we would like to transpire in our life, but we turn around and give ourselves all the reasons that won't happen. In essence, we are giving our unconscious mind mixed messages. When leading a workshop with church professionals, Roy will often ask how many people, when they need to get up at 6:00 a.m., can do that without setting an alarm clock. Usually 50 percent or more claim they can do this. Roy then asks a follow-up question: "What makes you wake up at 6:00 a.m.?" People rarely have an answer, but they know they can do it. One possible expla-nation is that they give their unconscious mind a direct message—"Wake me at 6:00"—and the brain takes over from there. There are always some people who say, "Yes, I can do this, but it usually means I wake up at 4:00 or 5:00 just to check if I haven't overslept." This usually means they have given themselves a direct message to "get me up at 6:00" but then say to themselves, "But maybe it won't work this time"—a mixed message.

Affirmations are always stated in positive language. Saying to your-self, "I'm not going to be afraid in the interview coming up today," is not an affirmation, because it suggests to the unconscious mind that fear can show up in that interview. An affirmation might be "The interview this afternoon will be a great opportunity for me to emphasize my gifts and strengths. I'm going to be positive and upbeat throughout the whole inter-view." Some people consciously write out affirmations, memorize them, and repeat them regularly. This can also be seen as a type of brain training in optimism.

Most congregations, particularly in liturgical denominations, use ritual and repetition, understanding that what we repeat becomes part of our identity. This could also be called a type of brain training. We the authors believe that we as Christians have an edge over others, because Christians' relationship with God prepares them for an optimistic life. This optimism is about more than life after death. It is a basic belief that we live in a benevolent universe and that God wants the best for us. An affirmation that would help us all if we repeated it every day is Psalm 23:

> The LORD is my shepherd, I shall not want. . . .
> my cup overflows.
> Surely goodness and mercy shall follow me all the days of my life, and I
> shall dwell in the house of the LORD my whole life long. (vv. 1, 5, 6)

Cultivation of a sense of gratitude contributes to the development of optimism. When we spend 60–80 percent of our waking time in gratitude, we are in an advanced state of optimism. We may feel grateful for things most people take for granted, such as having hot water for a shower in the morning. (Billions of people on this planet don't even have access to sanitary water.) We might enjoy orange juice splashing our tongue, having loving friends and family members, or living in a free country and feeling safe most of the time. *This* comes with brain training. It is an inside job. Regardless of our external circumstances, it is always possible to live in gratitude. Continuously practicing gratitude lays the groundwork for optimism. We continue to expect good things to happen to us. Consider the words to the song "Oh, what a beautiful mornin'" in *Oklahoma!*—when someone sings with confidence that "I've got a wonderful feelin', everything's goin' my way," their expectation is that the rest of their day will be great.

The more we exercise those parts of the brain that deal with positive emotions, the more positive emotion becomes the default way in which the brain functions—that is, the more it establishes a mood of optimism. This can always be a work in progress. All of us would experience a better life if we trained our brain to be more realistically optimistic.

Jesus and Optimism

In chapter 3, we saw that Jesus was an optimist or, to use different language, that he proclaimed a gospel of abundance. We cannot fully appreciate Jesus' abundance mentality unless we place it in its first-century context: the small village of Capernaum, Jesus' headquarters and home to subsistence peasant farmers and fishermen. It was a world of scarcity—poverty, disease, indebtedness, and the tensions that came with these realities. We can rightly call Jesus' abundance mentality "optimism," but we have to understand that it was an optimism rooted in Jesus' confidence in the unbounded graciousness of God, a God who is "kind to the ungrateful and the wicked" (Luke 6:35), who "makes his sun rise on the evil and on the good, and sends rain on the righteous and the unrighteous" (Matthew 5:45). Jesus taught his followers to think of God as a "father" whom they could trust to care for them.

Jesus firmly believed that God is a loving God who continually showers abundant blessings on us. He called followers who would themselves experience this reality by traveling from village to village without food, money, extra clothing, or even a staff with which to defend themselves (Matthew 10:5–10). They would be completely dependent upon the kindness of strangers and, through them, experience the care and goodness of God. Jesus assured them, "Ask, and it will be given you; search, and you will find; knock, and the door will be opened for you. For everyone who asks receives, and everyone who searches finds, and for everyone who knocks, the door will be opened" (Matthew 7:7–8). In reality, probably not every door was opened to them, but the doors were more likely to be open if the followers came with no agenda but to speak peace, cure the sick, and share the good news of a merciful and gracious God.

Jesus' gospel of a generous God challenged people to move beyond their normal worries, their scarcity mentality. He told his followers, "Do not worry about your life, what you will eat, or about your body, what you will wear" (Luke 12:22). "Consider the lilies, how they grow: they neither toil nor spin; yet I tell you, even Solomon in all his glory was not clothed like one of these" (Luke 12:27). After all, "your Father knows that you need them" (Luke 12:30), and God will provide. Jesus himself lived out of this confidence in God's care: he was a homeless man (Luke 9:58), dependent on others for everything, even a place to lay his head at night. This really goes beyond optimism as a hopeful attitude. Jesus trusted God with his life.

Although most early Christians no longer begged for a living, they expressed their trust in God through prayer, which was also based on an optimism rooted in trust. However, the radical dependence on God's care that we find in Jesus became evident again in the monastic movement, and the monks' example inspired many. Prayer, specifically petitionary prayer, continues to be based on confidence that God will care for God's people.

The opposite of an abundance mentality is a scarcity mentality. Jesus told a parable about a man with a scarcity mentality. Rather than expressing his gratitude to God by sharing his abundant crop, he chose to build more barns to store his surplus grain (Luke 12:16–20). When Jesus challenged his followers to give away their surplus—in fact, to give away everything (Mark 10:17–22; Luke 12:33)—he was challenging a scarcity mentality. Such a mentality lacks confidence that God will provide. Jesus was impressed by the widow who gave alms despite having almost nothing (Mark 12:41–44); this reflected an abundance mentality. She showed her confidence in God's goodness by giving out of her poverty, while the rich man, who proudly gave out of his abundance, did not demonstrate such confidence.

The most spectacular demonstration of God's abundant care, of course, is the story of the feeding of the multitudes. This story clearly made a deep impression in the early church because it is repeated, with variations, six times in the four Gospels.[10] Confronted by huge crowds that had come together in a desolate place, the disciples wanted to send the people away to towns where they might find food. Jesus asked what food people in the crowd had with them and was told of a boy who had two dried fish and five loaves of bread. "But what are these among so many?" the disciples asked. Jesus knew something the disciples did not: that God, beyond providing merely enough, would in fact provide an abundance—food for the multitude, plus twelve baskets more. This story is a vivid and inspiring demonstration of God's abundance.

To get a sense of how Jesus' kind of optimism might play out in the modern world, consider this example: Jesus' birthplace, Bethlehem, is today surrounded by very high walls built by Israel. The main industry, tourism, has suffered for years, and increasingly Israeli-led tours (mostly for Christian tourists) do not visit Bethlehem at all. Unemployment is very high. Residents of Bethlehem are not allowed to enter nearby Jerusalem or any part of Israel without special, scarce permits. Youth have very constricted futures. It is a place of scarcity, a virtual open prison.

In Bethlehem, a Palestinian Lutheran pastor, Mitri Raheb, has been inspired by John 10:10—"I came that they may have life, and have it abundantly." Arland knows Mitri personally, having been to Bethlehem many times and being very familiar with his philosophy. He and his colleagues have developed all kinds of programs—schools; medical clinics; training programs in tourism, the arts, and computers; and programs for children and women (e.g., the first Palestinian women's soccer team). He puts special emphasis on the arts. Why? Because the arts develop creativity, and creativity means unleashing imaginations, so young people can break free of their virtual prison and imagine a different, exciting future, one offering possibilities even right there living under occupation. The arts function in Bethlehem much like Jesus' parables in Capernaum, liberating people from their confinement and opening them to the kindness and surprising abundance of God. This unleashed creativity can include art exhibits, traveling dance troupes, documentary filmmaking, and creative activities for community children. These programs build confidence, and bring joy and hope that despite living under Israeli occupation and in the midst of scarcity, they can still "have life, and have it abundantly." Those inspired by Pastor Raheb's programs are fully aware of the difficulties and injustices they face, but they develop a defiant hope that is able to imagine an abundant life.

Pastor Raheb's example is instructive for congregations living under very different circumstances but too often with a scarcity mentality. Congregations need to stop thinking of what they *cannot* do and find ways to creatively challenge whatever scarcity mentality may keep them from living more abundant lives. Challenging the scarcity mentality of people in his day was Jesus' form of "optimism," the nurturing of an abundance mentality based on trust in God's care. Jesus created no programs, but his parables were able to break open the imagination of his people, his healing activity opened up new life for those hobbled by illness, and his fearless embrace even of enemies modeled the indiscriminate graciousness of God.

Conclusion

We have seen that optimism—which is not merely viewing the world through rose-colored glasses—is an essential part of emotional intelligence. Relationships among people are going to be much more productive and enjoyable if the people involved are optimistic rather than pessimistic. Confronted by obstacles or failure, they will be more resilient because they expect that they will learn from their failures and obstacles, and move on. Optimism tends to be contagious. Congregations with optimistic leadership are likely to be more productive and certainly more enjoyable than congregations infected with fear, anxiety, and pessimism.

We saw that we can train our brains to be optimistic or pessimistic. Fear is a particularly noxious emotion, and it erodes optimism and destroys joy.

Jesus was optimistic. He believed and lived out a confidence in the graciousness and care of a fatherly God. Congregations that share this theology of abundance will be generous, caring, and hopeful. They will not focus mainly on what they lack, or on their debts, but rather on the abundance that God has provided and continues to give them.

SEVEN

Stress Resilience and Jesus

S tress resilience is the ability to face difficult and even frightening situations without breaking down physically, losing one's capacity to focus, or becoming ineffective in accomplishing the task at hand. Being able to manage one's stress is a necessary skill if one wants to be competent in a chosen career and also have a joyful private life. As the rate of change in the world continues to accelerate, the trait of stress resilience becomes even more central to life and health.

Currently, EQ literature lists this trait as stress tolerance. We, the authors, think that someone who is catatonic can be stress tolerant, as can someone who is completely oblivious to the realities of life. Stress resilience more closely identifies what we believe this EQ trait is all about.

Within congregational life, internal conflict appears to generate the most stress in both staff and members. Yet healthy congregational conflict is necessary for personal spiritual development as well as congregational growth. Without such conflict, members do not grow spiritually and the entire congregation will remain stuck in the past.

On a personal level, we need to be able to embrace our darkness. In Jungian terms, we need to become acquainted with our shadow and come to own it, which is our rejected self that we have suppressed into our unconscious. Our shadow is the part of ourselves that makes excuses for why we are not more caring, more generous, more committed to trying to serve the mission of the church. Facing into our darker side is often experienced as internal conflict. It is where we need to experience personal conflict by associating with a congregation that has the wisdom, insight, and courage to help us face into this aspect of ourselves. We need to say, with the hymn, "just as I am, without one plea."

Mother Teresa is often described as not having a very high opinion of herself. She did not see herself as the "saint" engaged in her ministry among the street people of Calcutta. Embracing our shadow side gives us a profound sense of humility—which more accurately characterized her. She clung desperately to the mercy and grace of God. The way she left her life here on the earth is interesting. When the whole world was mourning the tragic death of Princess Diana, she quietly slipped away. Even in death, it seems, she did not want people to ever make a big deal about her and her ministry.

In short, a spiritual teacher needs to inject conflict into a disciple's life. Without conflict, we remain at levels of immaturity and don't grow spiritually. The conflict is likely asking us the question, "When are you going to grow up?" Jesus was consistently challenging his disciples by confronting them with their levels of immaturity. Within congregational life, there needs to be a kind of psychological contract between pastor and people that "sometimes I'm going to make you quite uncomfortable in my sermons and in my personal conversations with you." We should not accept spiritual messages that just always make us feel good about ourselves—a feel-good gospel. That is going to keep us stuck at immature levels of self-insight.

In order for congregations to grow, both numerically and spiritually, we will need to experience conflict at all levels of congregational life. We want people to come to meetings to fight hard for what they believe should be our mission and ministry. Without conflict, there is little creativity in church meetings. This means learning to live with the stress that this kind of conflict implies. When people fight hard for their ideas, there are going to be arguments to the contrary. If we are always "nice" to one another, little of inspirational value is going to occur in meetings.

The Mechanisms of Stress

Through the millennia, our bodies have evolved from more primitive states, but basic survival mechanisms are still in place. Whenever we are threatened, our bodies get ready for either fight or flight. The threat may not even be physical. We might sense that our self-esteem or dignity is being threatened if we are treated unjustly or rudely. Our brain has two walnut-sized components, one on each side of our brain, called the amygdala, that store every frightening experience we have ever had. If the amygdala senses stimuli similar to those present in a previous wounding, it sends a warning to our two prefrontal lobes, which are a type of control center, and we have about six seconds to determine whether this threat is similar to an earlier frightening experience or not. The decision-making part of our brain, mainly our two prefrontal lobes, can shut down in a full-fledged fight/flight/freeze response. If it doesn't do this within six seconds, our brain goes on full alert for something stressful to happen. It sends a signal to the adrenal gland atop the kidney, which in turn triggers the secretion of the hormones epinephrine and norepinephrine. When they hit, adrenaline is pumped into our bloodstream. Suddenly, a surge flows through the entire body, priming it for an emergency. When these chemicals hit the body, our blood pressure rises, our heart starts to beat faster, our pupils dilate, our stomach stops digesting food, and the liver dumps a bunch of sugar into the bloodstream, all getting the body ready for fight/flight or freeze. In primitive times, the main question when confronted by such a situation was "Does it eat me or do I eat it?" Today the questions that come upon us in a stressful situation are much more complex: "Is this going to cost me my job?" "Will I lose a loved one because of this situation?" "Is my integrity being assaulted here?"

This primitive response to threat has saved the lives of humans for thousands of years. This same mechanism, which can save our lives, becomes less functional in the twenty-first century, when fighting and running are most likely not appropriate. Often, the threats we experience are not physical but emotional. We might sense that our self-esteem or dignity is being threatened if we are treated unjustly or rudely, insulted, or demeaned. Within a congregation, a pastor might be accused of not doing her job properly in a church board meeting. To run/fight or freeze physically would be a sure sign of incompetence. What she might like to do is smack someone in the mouth or simply leave the room, but neither option would convince other board members that she is competent. So, even though this torrent is raging through her body, she may try to listen and respond appropriately. She might try to say as calmly as possible, "Well, tell me more," and then try to actively listen to the person lodging the complaint.

Responses to Stress

In the mid-1960s, social scientists Thomas Holmes and Richard Rahe devised a rating scale that assigned point values to numerous stressful experiences, to determine whether it would be possible to identify a correlation between stress and illness among five thousand patients.[1] They theorized that any time we are confronted with something new or novel, our stress level goes up a notch. Any one of these novel events, by themselves, might not trigger in our bodies the symptoms of stress, but the accumulation of many life-changing events at one time could tip the balance, and it will show up somehow, somewhere in our bodies. Many of the items on their scale have to do with a loss of some kind—loss of a spouse, a job, a house, money, and so forth. Each item is given a numerical rating, depending upon its importance to the person. (If you would like to take the survey, it is available in appendix II.) However, Holmes and Rahe could not say that a certain number of life-changing events would put everyone into a stress state, because people respond to stress differently. Some people remain calm even when a dozen things are going haywire in their lives, while other people can't handle even a few disruptions.

An individual experiences negative effects only when his or her personal threshold for stress tolerance is surpassed. Everyone's threshold is different. This is where another survey developed by John Adams, called the "Strain Response Inventory,"[2] can help us determine whether we have surpassed our threshold level of stress. All it does is identify physical symptoms such as headaches, heartburn, feeling nervous, inability to sleep, loss of interest in sex, or needing more sex than ever.

We know we are over our own threshold level of stress when too many body symptoms appear. In the Strain Response Inventory, a score of 21 or higher is a good indication that you are over your threshold level of stress. A score of 31 or higher means you are way over your threshold level. These also are different in each individual. Some people get headaches; others get upset stomachs or sweaty palms. Other symptoms are shortness of breath, feeling unhealthy, back problems, misdirected anger, excessive use of alcohol or drugs, high blood pressure, suicidal thoughts, difficulty getting out of bed in the morning, loss of appetite, and so forth. Our bodies are going to tell us we are over our stress threshold. When our self-awareness is so low, however, that we remain oblivious to these physical symptoms, we are a disaster waiting to happen. Should you want to take this survey yourself, go to appendix III.

To stay at a constant state of readiness to fight or run is physically exhausting. We are going to wear our body out by having adrenaline continuously coursing through our veins. Hence, we need to develop coping strategies that minimize the long-term destructive effects of stress responses on our physical and emotional life.

At first, our bodies will give us simple messages—such as a whispered "Slow down." If we don't listen, it will speak more loudly. If we still don't listen, it will shout. A shout could be a heart attack, cancer, stroke, or other major health issue. There is a saying that "death is nature's way of telling us to slow down."

Stress resilience is a trait of emotional intelligence because it helps us manage our emotions better. It takes considerable skill to maintain equilibrium and a state of calm amid life's stresses. Anyone hoping to excel in a given vocation will need to manage one's stress. When stress gets the better of us, we are regarded as less capable, if not incompetent. For example, someone who has frequent meltdowns in meetings, in the form of either angry outbursts or breaking into tears, is going to be seen as emotionally immature. Someone who has an excessively high number of sick days at work may be a person who can't handle the stress of his or her job.

We have discussed an amygdala hijack in earlier chapters. People who have excessive numbers of hijacks as adults will not exhibit mature emotional control in public. Possibly someone has had a dysfunctional family life involving much violence in the growing-up years. For this person to grow in emotional intelligence, he will need to demonstrate greater emotional control in his life if he is to experience a successful career or satisfying personal life.

Self-awareness is key to stress resilience. Self-awareness enables us to pay attention to the way events affect our emotions, our thoughts, and our body. With self-awareness, we can begin to practice self-care coping strategies. We can also become aware of what types of self-care work best for us in any given moment or environment. If we fail to follow personal disciplines that keep us calm and centered, life will continue to be a challenge.

The trait of self-confidence also plays a big part in stress resilience. Whenever we feel unable to meet a certain challenge, our stress level jumps higher. If we continually tell ourselves that we are not able to manage stressful events, we can "catastrophize" them, making them even more overwhelming. With self-confidence, we have the possibility of becoming more stress resilient. Life and its challenges never remain overwhelming for very long, helping us avoid getting locked into fear and anxiety.

Jesus and Stress

The Gospels portray Jesus as a person of great equanimity. Whether confronted by crowds, opponents, or unhappy family members, he always seems in possession of himself. When a storm arises on the Sea of Galilee, he is the picture of calm, sleeping in the boat (Mark 4:35–41).

Words that describe an ability to tolerate stress are absent from the Gospels, including words such as "unperturbed," "composed," "serene," "tranquil," and "self-controlled." However, we also cannot we find words that describe Jesus as anxious under stress. Of course, it is possible to tolerate stress by being indifferent to the pain and struggles of others, or by simply being stoic, resigned, or compliant. Jesus is not portrayed this way. He does warn against even basic worries such as food and clothing (Matthew 6:25–34). Luke is the one who especially emphasizes how Jesus withdrew from the crowds (Luke 5:16; 9:10; 22:41; cf. Mark 6:30), which is a healthy way of dealing with stress. Jesus is portrayed as unflappable in the presence of opponents, the many ill, and others. Even confronted by the devil in the wilderness, he seems not only unflappable but also assertive (Matthew 4:1–11/Luke 4:1–13).

Jesus did provide advice to his disciples about how to deal with certain stressful situations, such as being accused (Matthew 5:25) or assaulted by those who are able to kill only the body, not the soul (Matthew 10:28) or when being prosecuted for some reason (Matthew 10:19–20/Luke 12:11–12). His followers are to pray that they not be led to the test (Matthew 6:13). If being the "salt of the earth" implies a certain pluckiness or boldness, then this is what Jesus recommends (Matthew 5:13). In Matthew 11:28–30, Jesus issues an invitation to "Come to me, all you that are weary and are carrying heavy burdens, and I will give you rest." At Gethsemane, Jesus struggled with his fate and prayed to be spared (Matthew 26:42), but the account of his "agony" in which his sweat fell like great drops of blood is a later addition to Luke.[3]

To actually follow Jesus is a great challenge and can be stressful. To love our enemies is a real stress test. To forgive those who have violated us places us under stress, even as the act of forgiveness frees us from damaging emotions. Even though most of us may not be called upon to stand steady in the midst of a storm, the challenges of discipleship can be daunting. But Jesus did not shrink from asking his followers to accept such difficult challenges as loving our enemies or being the salt of the earth, nor did he minimize the difficulties. Jesus called us to trust our Father who will care for us and sustain us in our journey. A well-known prayer captures this courage in the face of uncertainty: "Lord God, you have called your servants to ventures of which we cannot see the ending, by paths as yet untrodden, through perils unknown. Give us faith to go out with good courage, not knowing where we go, but only that your hand is leading us and your love supporting us; through Jesus Christ our Lord."[4]

A life without stress is not to be desired, as we would not encounter the stimuli to keep us on a growing edge—yet neither is a life that is continually overwhelmed by stress to be desired. We believe that Jesus provides us with a great example of how to live within these two extremes.

EIGHT

Loving One's Enemies and Jesus

Loving Enemies as Emotional Intelligence

As we review the EQ traits developed by authors and EQ survey developers, we cannot help but raise the question: Are there any that are missing? Given our Judeo-Christian heritage, in which relationships with others hold a special sacred place in our lives, what EQ traits might be added to those identified in previous chapters? We claim there are two: love of our enemies and forgiveness.

Jesus famously commanded his audience to love their enemies. This is a complex and psychologically insightful command. It requires great emotional intelligence and, as we will see, has surprisingly direct implications for life in a congregation.

What Jesus Said

You have heard that it was said, "An eye for an eye and a tooth for a tooth." But I say to you, Do not resist an evildoer. But if anyone strikes you on the right cheek, turn the other also; and if anyone wants to sue you and take your coat, give your cloak as well; and if anyone forces you to go one mile, go also the second mile. Give to everyone who begs from you, and do not refuse anyone who wants to borrow from you.

You have heard that it was said, "You shall love your neighbor and hate your enemy." But I say to you, Love your enemies and pray for those who persecute you, so that you may be children of your Father in heaven; for he makes his sun rise on the evil and on the good, and sends rain on the righteous and on the unrighteous. For if you love those who love you, what reward do you have? Do not even the tax collectors do the same? And if you greet only your brothers and sisters, what more are you doing than others? Be perfect, therefore, as your heavenly Father is perfect. (Matthew 5:38–48)[1]

In Matthew, the relevant section begins with the explicit rejection of the ancient law of retaliation (*lex talionis*). This law evolved to limit revenge, which easily gets out of control, as powerfully illustrated in the story of Lamech in Genesis 4:19–24. An eye for an eye and a tooth for a tooth is not a sign of primitive bloodthirstiness. It was an effort to make retaliation proportional and to limit the socially disruptive nature of unlimited revenge, which can quickly become a whirlpool of violence, pulling others into its vortex.

It is very important at the outset that we consider the nature of revenge. We do not regard revenge as inherently evil or evidence of sinfulness. Revenge is a product of human evolution. The powerful instinct to take revenge when being wronged is often seen as the root of our sense of, and demand for, justice. It can be protective of society if taking revenge can restrain the violent. To take revenge is to assert one's dignity and worth in the face of actions or words by those who would demean, violate, and treat one as unworthy of being treated as the victimizer would wish to be treated. It is to refuse to accept mistreatment by others. But, as we noted, revenge easily gets out of control.

The failure to take revenge can be very negative. For example, instead of taking revenge, the victim might become merely passive or may harbor such anger and resentment that the victim may erupt destructively. Or the victim may internalize the shame of being unable to resist being victimized. This might happen, for example, with rape and domestic abuse victims. People who have experienced humiliation will often withdraw from others and isolate themselves, fearing further humiliation, and such isolation is itself dangerous because it allows the stew pot of anger and rage to continue to boil.

The Power of Revenge Lies in the Experience of Humiliation

Our very dignity, our honor, our sense of self-respect can be destroyed by many kinds of violations of our person. The injury need not be physical at all. If the shaming is public, the desire for revenge will be especially powerful. Our honor is more valuable to us than anything else because it is our very identity, but it is completely dependent upon others' recognition or attribution to us of honor and respect. These dynamics apply equally to individuals and to groups, including nations. Increasingly, we are seeing studies that explore the role of humiliation in such areas as in triggering wars and international conflict,[2] fueling the Israeli-Palestinian conflict,[3] motivating terrorism,[4] forming the fundamentalist mind-set,[5] and shaping China's recent policies.[6] Humiliation is almost certainly deeply implicated in congregational conflicts. In fact, it is likely that many conflicts in congregations have little to do with what the conflict appears to be about; rather, they arise from experiences of humiliation, rejection, or other perceived slights.

Matthew and Luke both record Jesus' injunction to love enemies (Luke 6:27; Matthew 5:44). Each lists several kinds of "enemies" to illustrate the concrete meaning of loving enemies. One of these examples does not seem to be an enemy—namely, the beggar (Matthew 5:42/Luke 6:30)—but three others listed by Matthew are the kinds of personal antagonists peasants would have encountered: the *slave master*, who strikes you on the cheek (Matthew 5:39b), the *state functionary*, who demands that you carry his things (Matthew 5:41), and the *creditor*, who sues you for nonpayment of a loan (Matthew 5:40). These examples clearly relate to a specific context: the peasants of Galilee in their struggles to survive in the face of superiors. In fact, these three are likely to have been the primary sources of the oppression of peasants. They are not simply personal antagonists. The enemies Jesus mentions are people who can use their positions of relative power to humiliate peasants by slapping them, treating them as beasts of burden, and demanding payment. These were much more insults to the peasants' dignity and honor than they were physically abusive. From the point of view of those subjected to these actions, they would have been acts of public humiliation, violations of their dignity.

It is very important to recognize that the behaviors that Jesus describes were *socially sanctioned* behaviors that would have been seen as normal in a hierarchical society. The master had every right, in that society, to punish or discipline a servant or slave. A creditor had every right to sue for nonpayment of a loan. A state functionary had the right to compel subjects to perform a wide variety of tasks. Given the way society was ordered, these were entirely normal acts, not simply fits of anger or violations of social norms. They were not illegitimate exercises of power. By calling for creative, nonviolent resistance to these actions, Jesus was also rejecting the social norms that legitimated such behaviors and was counseling nonviolent resistance to peasant oppression.

Walter Wink has provided a creative and persuasive interpretation of this text, preferring the wording in Matthew 5:38–41. In what follows, I am indebted to his work, though not all of the details are from Wink's study. Wink has shown that the text actually involves gestures that aim to transform the enemy.[7] He calls these acts of "subversive assertiveness." The formulations in both Matthew and Luke are impersonal (e.g., "the ones who . . ."), but the identity of the "enemies" is easily discerned.

In the first example, a person (no doubt, a slave owner or superior) uses his right hand to give a *backhanded slap* to the right cheek of the other person. By slapping the slave or servant, he was insulting him, demeaning him. The slave is advised to "turn the other cheek"—that is, the left cheek, which would require the master's next blow to be from his right fist. The use of a fist would imply that the slave is an equal, in spite of the violence entailed. By turning his cheek, the slave is choosing not to be passive, but rather to dare the master to treat him as an equal and to hit him with his fist. The slave is to refuse to be insulted and to demand his dignity as an equal.

In the second example, the context is a demand for a peasant debtor to pay off a loan, presumably a loan with exorbitant interest or other fraudulent element. Indebtedness was a major problem in the Galilee of Jesus' day.[8] Since the peasant has no money, the judge demands his outer garment (Greek: *himation*).[9] Jesus advises the hapless peasant to remove his tunic (Greek: *chitōn*) as well and give it to the creditor, leaving the peasant stark naked, a taboo in that society and an embarrassment to the creditor, who would be left standing in front of the debtor's home holding both garments. The peasant has chosen to confront his accuser by taking the initiative.

In the third example, someone, perhaps a soldier or functionary of the state, has demanded that a peasant carry his load for one mile. This action was sanctioned by a widespread practice in which superiors, especially those performing some function related to the state, could compel service by subjects.[10] The peasant is told to insist on going two miles, throwing the superior off balance and taking the initiative himself. He is now the actor. He refuses to be humiliated by the superior and insists on seeing this as voluntary service that he is happy to perform.

As we noted earlier, these are examples of humiliating actions by superiors toward their inferiors. Jesus' suggested responses would have had the effect of evoking laughter from his peasant listeners, humor that would encourage them to actually be courageous and creative in resisting oppression—nonviolently, since the power differential was so vast that using violence would have been stupid. In other words, we can see the creative responses that Jesus suggests as empowering. These examples also assume that the oppressors do have a modicum of human decency and that they can be challenged to act upon it. As we will see for forgiveness, love of enemies entails the recognition of the humanity of the enemy, his ability to recognize the injustice of his behavior and to change, though the strategy could be empowering for the peasant involved even if the superior failed to change.

Jesus' admonition to love the enemy is linked in both Matthew and Luke with various positive behaviors: praying for one's persecutors, doing good to those who hate, blessing those who curse, and so forth. This tells us that loving the enemy is clearly and explicitly aimed at *the transformation of the perpetrator*. Paul's series of ethical injunctions in Romans 12 reflects this same idea: love of enemies is an active love, an effort to rise above enmity and humiliation, and to seek the transformation of the enemy.[11]

It seems that Jesus understood very well that revenge is rooted in humiliation. But the examples show that Jesus was not simply calling for the renunciation of revenge. He was calling for actions on the part of peasants that required summoning up courage and refusing to have their dignity impugned. These actions might lead to the transformation of the victimizers, but even if they did not, they would be healthy, self-affirming, empowering acts of nonviolent resistance to oppression. Moreover, Jesus communicated clearly that he refused to accept as normal the social structures that legitimated the humiliation of peasants. The actions assume that the humiliators have some feeling for others, some empathy, that might be awakened by startling responses to their probably entrenched sense of entitlement and resulting expressions of arrogant mistreatment of others.

Of course, other strategies might be appropriate in situations in which the imbalance of power was less stark.

The dynamics and potential results of humiliation and revenge require further consideration. Humiliation is erosive of one's dignity, and the responses can be anger and rage, isolation and cutting oneself off from others, conflict and violence. These are not always the results, but we argue that many conflicts have their roots in humiliation of various kinds.

The nation has been subjected to wrenching stories of mass killings in recent years. In a study of "The Social Psychology of Humiliation and Revenge," Bettina Muenster and David Lotto discuss the killer of twenty-seven students and five teachers at Virginia Tech in 2007. They say, "Consumed by rage over the way society treated him and evidently feeling like an outsider who did not get the respect he deserved, he chose solitude and seemed invisible for most of his life. In fact he had no social bonds whatsoever."[12] They go on to say that "recent studies on school shootings reveal some astonishingly common characteristics: except for one of fifteen investigated, all shooters were male; a majority experienced chronic or acute humiliation, mostly through more or less cruel rejection and social exclusion by others; many exhibited narcissistic tendencies; and most had an obsession with firearms and explosives."[13] A *New York Times* article on Adam Lanza, who on December 14, 2012, killed twenty first graders, six teachers, his mother, and himself in Newtown, Connecticut, provided a portrait of Lanza that had emerged by late March 2013 that had a very similar cluster of characteristics: a young man who felt bullied and disrespected and who isolated himself.[14]

Mass killers are, of course, extreme examples. But it is almost inescapable that every congregation contains people with varying degrees of feeling rejected, demeaned, slighted, publicly shamed, humiliated, or having their worth not acknowledged. Some members will have lost jobs or applied many times for jobs and been rejected. Some youth with an intense need of acceptance by peers will have experienced rejection or at least lack of acceptance. Others children will have been bullied. There will be women (and men) who have suffered domestic abuse or rape. Some members might feel slighted by the pastor or other members. The pastor herself may have felt slighted or demeaned by things people in the congregation have said or done. It is likely that some of the conflicts in the congregation are not really what they appear to be about. Members may drop out because they feel excluded or at least not recognized.

So how does love of enemies translate in the parish? Here "enemies" means people who have become antagonistic, especially as a result of humiliation. We can suggest practices that might address issues of humiliation in the congregation. It must be recognized that the experience of humiliation is not only powerful but also long lasting, and that it will *not* go away on its own. Only specific interventions to acknowledge the pain and its causes, and to restore self-respect and dignity, will be able to address the profound effects of humiliation. In this respect, understanding and promoting forgiveness will be crucial but must not be done cavalierly as if people could simply forgive and forget. Superficial forgiveness may be worse than no forgiveness.

Church staffs need to understand the dynamics of humiliation, shame, and dignity and learn to become sensitive to the possible deeper roots of conflict in the congregation. Congregations need to develop a strong sense of community, treating all with equal respect, and especially reaching out to embrace and include the estranged and isolated. Forgiveness of self and of others needs to be taught. In the New Testament, a constant refrain for the development and maintenance of community is humility, not thinking too highly of oneself, willing to acknowledge the worth even of people one does not like.[15] These are especially important because they are countercultural.

The notion of loving one's enemies is also counterintuitive. Whether in national or local discourse, the identification and demonization of all kinds of enemies are seen as perfectly normal discourse. Too often, individuals, groups, and nations prop up their self-worth by devaluing others, by defining themselves by what they are not. Behavior that is demeaning to others is often accepted in society, as numerous complaints of police harassment suggest. Many Americans seemed quite willing to accept the torture of people at Guantanamo because they did not consider the prisoners as their equals. Often the poor are thought to deserve their fate. American culture is highly competitive, including in the areas of respect, fame, and rankings.

To love one's enemies is to reject the demonization of the enemy, to affirm the humanity of the enemy, and to acknowledge the possibility that the enemy can change. Loving one's enemies also means refusing to *be* an enemy. Moreover, loving one's enemy means committing oneself to a *relationship* with the enemy, which is why the word "love" is used. It is, in a way, a very aggressive act. It means, in fact, launching an offensive with all the creative tools at one's disposal to challenge the enemy, to appeal to whatever human values the enemy might profess, to do everything possible to alter the behavior of the enemy. The EQ trait of assertiveness is essential to loving one's enemies, as are other EQ traits such as impulse control and self-awareness. These clearly must have been traits that Jesus himself understood and possessed.

Nonviolent Resistance

Many readers will recognize what love of enemies describes on the transpersonal level: nonviolent resistance. Gandhi and Martin Luther King Jr. are only the most famous of the advocates of nonviolent resistance. For them, nonviolence did not mean simply being nice and avoiding violence, piously keeping oneself unstained by violent acts. It meant devising every creative way one could imagine—short of violence itself—to change the behavior, if not the whole mentality, of the oppressor. Nonviolent resistance is not the only way to express of love of enemies, but it is a particularly powerful example, and one that has been studied at great length.[16] It is the tactic of oppressed minorities, those who are powerless, being exploited, humiliated, and abused.

Some of the most poignant and powerful examples of loving the enemy have come from, of all places, Palestine. Maxine Kaufman-Lacusta provides numerous examples and analyses of both Palestinian and Israeli citizen nonviolent resistance to the onerous Israeli occupation of the West Bank.[17]

An especially poignant example is a Palestinian doctor in Gaza, Izzeldin Abuelaish, who lost three daughters and a cousin during the three-week Israeli siege of Gaza beginning December 27, 2008. His house, containing only his family and no munitions or Hamas militants, was attacked. Another daughter lost a finger and the sight in one eye. Sadly, this was not the first tragedy for the family. His wife, Nadia, had died of leukemia just months before. His family had also fled their village in 1948, fearing Zionist attacks on Arabs. The family farm was later owned by the late Ariel Sharon, who also had ordered the demolition of the family's home in Gaza in 1970. Israel has refused to apologize for killing his daughters. But Dr. Abuelaish, a Muslim, has told his family's story both in speeches and in a book titled *I Shall Not Hate: A Gaza Doctor's Journey*.[18] He told reporter Rachel Cooke, "I do not believe in revenge; hatred is an illness, and the enemy of peace."[19] Many other such stories could be told. In fact, there is a long history of nonviolent resistance in Palestine.[20]

What Love of Enemies Is *Not*

By now, it should be clear, in our view, what love of enemies is *not*:

- It is not a nice and high ideal that is impossible in real life.
- It does not entail ignoring the threat posed by your enemy.
- It does not mean "liking" your enemy.
- It does not mean just being nice to your enemy.
- It does not mean accepting what your enemy does.

Loving the Enemy Within

Roy sees another dimension to Jesus' teaching about loving the enemy. His analysis helps us think about a very important process—namely, the process by which we demonize our enemies. He also suggests how we might overcome this destructive tendency. As Roy shows, understanding how this process works is part of emotional intelligence, if we desire to be truly loving and peaceful people. In these cases, an enemy may simply be someone in our church or work setting whom we have a hard time accepting.

Projection

The therapeutic community worldwide has generally accepted projection theory. According to this theory, we cannot really know another person completely, so we put together our projections of them based on whatever sensate data we have and on our own emotional needs. This is true for people we like and as well as those we dislike.

The therapeutic community claims we have a tendency to project our darker impulses onto other people. We know these dark impulses are wrong, but we cannot accept them and instead unconsciously project them onto others. We confirm our worth, our virtue, by attributing these feelings to others. When we suppress these dark impulses, they don't really go away. They remain stored in the unconscious in what Carl Jung called our shadow self.

Roy suggests that by calling us to love our enemies, Jesus was encouraging us to reel in our prejudices and projections, owning them as being more about us than our enemy. This is most clearly expressed in Matthew 7:1–5, where Jesus says:

Do not judge, so that you may not be judged. For with the judgment
you make you will be judged, and the measure you give will be the
measure you get. Why do you see the speck in your neighbor's eye,
but do not notice the log in your own eye? Or how can you say to
your neighbor, "Let me take the speck out of your eye," while the
log is in your own eye? You hypocrite, first take the log out of your
own eye, and then you will see clearly to take the speck out of your
neighbor's eye.

Jesus understood the phenomenon of human projection. He warns us
about the danger of our being critical of others, because we may be blind
to our own need for reform, our own prejudices.

Emotional intelligence entails coming to terms with our shadow material and coming to accept all people with grace and equanimity. In short,
it means to confront our prejudices, all of them, and accept them for being
just that—prejudices.

Roy knows a female Lutheran pastor who for years fought the
church's desire to be more accepting of gays and lesbians. It was not until
she had an epiphany, much like the light of truth hitting Saul of Tarsus on
his way to Damascus, that she realized that she, herself, was a lesbian. This
epiphany took place some thirty years ago, when being gay was considered
repulsive by most within our culture. In those days, when a boy or girl
noticed any sort of affection toward someone of the same sex, that would
have been suppressed as quickly and deeply as possible. This woman felt it
was an important part of her mission as a Christian to condemn homosex-
ual behavior wherever possible. She was vilifying a part of herself that she
was projecting onto others. Her "conversion" in this case came as a shot
right through her heart. This is not an uncommon story. Given the strong
taboo about homosexuality in the past, thousands of people suppressed
this tendency in themselves, marrying and having kids, trying their best to
lead a straight life, and only coming to own that side of themselves much
later in life. This is not to say that everyone who despises homosexuals is
suppressing this tendency in oneself, but in some cases this is true.

Country-western singer Kris Kristofferson has a song called "Jesus
Was a Capricorn," in which the chorus talks about everyone having someone to look down on, which makes them feel better about themselves. In
the last line of the chorus, he proposes that if people can't find someone to
look down on, they look down on him instead. In this line, Kristofferson
is posing as a Christ figure upon whom people may project their shadow

material. Racial and cultural prejudices allow those who buy into them the ability to feel better than someone else.

How do we address this tendency in all of us? Not easily. In fact, it takes hard, intentional work. Yet most psychotherapists would say this is an important step to take toward spiritual and emotional health. Whether in the church or secular workplace, moving to this level of maturity is necessary if we are to function with emotional intelligence. Within a context of safety and trust, we may be able to gain insight into the ways we are projecting our own bad stuff onto others.

What can our enemy give us that no one else can? Right! Our enemies have the potential to be a mirror for us to see the part of our rejected self that we are projecting onto them. They may be the key to our moving toward health and wholeness—that is, owning our projections. It can be a humbling experience coming to this realization. It is the pathway to radical self-acceptance.

Neither "forgiveness" nor "loving one's enemies" typically figures into books on emotional intelligence, but we believe that they both need to be seen as important traits or capacities if one is to be truly emotionally intelligent. We urge those who study emotional intelligence to do research on these powerful human capacities, even exploring the possibility that neuroscience might help us understand them more deeply.

NINE

Forgiveness and Jesus

Forgiveness as Emotional Intelligence

The discoverer of forgiveness in the realm of human affairs was Jesus of Nazareth.

—Hannah Arendt, *The Human Condition*

In October 2006, a man entered a small Amish school near Lancaster, Pennsylvania, barricaded himself inside, and shot ten Amish schoolgirls, killing five of them. The man had allowed a pregnant woman, three parents of infants, and fifteen boys to leave the school unharmed; one girl escaped along with her mother. The killer, Charles Roberts, a milk-truck driver who lived in the area, then killed himself. The massacre made the national news, of course, but what shocked many even more was the fact that the Amish soon after forgave the killer and went to visit the killer's wife, three children, and parents to comfort them. Some of the Amish went to the funeral for the killer, and others set up a charitable fund to support the Roberts family. Some people were offended by the way the Amish reacted. Others were simply amazed and admired the courage and compassion of the Amish. Later, it was learned that nine years earlier, a daughter of the Robertses had died twenty minutes after she was born; Roberts was never able to forgive God for that. For years he had been tormented about this. Apparently, in his twisted mind, he had decided that if his daughter could not live, other daughters would not live, either.[1]

Usually, mass killings like this are followed by expressions of recrimination and calls to take steps to prevent such violence in the future. Hatred is expressed against the killer or killers. Anger is common. But, inspired by the teaching of Jesus, these Amish forgave the killer of their children, and then they went beyond that to help the killer's wife and family.

Jesus gave a prominent role to forgiveness. In the Lord's Prayer (Matthew 6:9–13/Luke 11:2–4), bread and forgiveness are coupled together as the basic human needs. Moreover, divine forgiveness is linked to interpersonal forgiveness: "Forgive us our sins, for we ourselves forgive everyone indebted to us" (Luke 11:4). By "interpersonal forgiveness," we mean forgiveness involving two individuals or groups, the victim(s) and the offender(s).

The word used in the Gospels that is translated as "forgiveness" is *aphesis*, which means release from, pardon, or cancellation of an obligation. The related verb translated "forgive" is *aphiæmi*, which means to let go, send away, cancel, remit, pardon, leave behind. The act of forgiveness is an act of letting go, a canceling of obligations, freeing oneself from something. The vivid metaphor of canceling a debt was used in the Lord's Prayer and captures a basic quality of forgiveness. A woman whose husband had been murdered after a musical performance when he stopped to help a man whose car had stopped along a highway commented that you just have to let go of the loss. Otherwise, she said, you can't go on.

That God forgives is often mentioned in the Old Testament, but it is almost exclusively a divine prerogative.[2] It was the temple cult that had a monopoly on the dispensing of forgiveness. Did Jesus move beyond that understanding of forgiveness? We believe that we can see breakthroughs in several texts indicating a movement toward a different understanding of forgiveness, one focusing on interpersonal forgiveness.

The first breakthrough occurs in the story of a young paralytic lad let down through the roof of a house because those carrying him could not even get close to the front door (Mark 2:1–12/Matthew 9:1–8/Luke 5:17–26). Seeing their "faith" (in Jesus as healer) demonstrated by their dramatic entry, Jesus says, "Son,[3] your sins are forgiven." The assumption in the story is that the child's paralysis was due to sin, either his own or his family's. The assumption was that releasing the child from his sin would also unbind the child's limbs, but of course it is also assumed that only God can release the child from his crippling sin. "Some scribes" nearby wonder, "Who can forgive sins but God alone?" Jesus responds to their murmuring: "'So that you may know that the Son of Man has authority to forgive sins'—he said to the paralytic—'I say to you, stand up, take your mat and go to your home.'" The healing proves that sin was forgiven. The NRSV capitalizes the words "Son of Man," implying that this is a claim to divine authority. However, "son of man" need not be understood as anything more than "a human being," which, in fact, is how Matthew apparently understood it, because he says that the crowds marveled that God "had given such authority to human beings"[4] (Matthew 9:8). The breakthrough here is the claim that humans may assume God's role and forgive sins. If this were an isolated text, we would be hesitant to claim a breakthrough, but, as we shall see, it is not. In fact, we can envision a trajectory moving from this text to sayings such as John 20:23: "If you forgive the sins of any, they are forgiven them [by God]." This is an explicit claim that human acts of forgiveness are, in effect, divine acts of forgiveness.

This breakthrough has the potential to eliminate the role of the temple cult in dispensing forgiveness and can give an almost transcendent role to interpersonal relationships. Of course, the later church has had a tendency to reclaim a monopoly on the authority to dispense divine forgiveness. On the other hand, the authority to forgive can also be trivialized and lose its seriousness and become cheap grace. We will see that, at least in Matthew's community, this did not happen.

A second breakthrough comes in Matthew 18:21–22/Luke 17:4. In Matthew, Peter asks how often he should forgive someone: seven times? No, says Jesus, "not seven times, but, I tell you, seventy-seven times." Matthew's version is more radical than Luke's in two respects. First, in Luke forgiveness is commanded in response to the repentance of the offender. In Matthew, nothing is said of the other person repenting. Forgiveness there appears to be unconditional. Second, in Luke one is to forgive seven times. Matthew's version actually sounds like a correction of Luke's version: not seven times, but seventy-seven! But even Luke's version may be radical: repentance there is directed to humans, not to God. That Matthew does not neglect repentance is evident from his more elaborate rule for how to deal with a member of the congregation who sins (Matthew 18:15–17), but there, too, forgiveness is declared by humans, acting under the authority of God. This, in fact, is made explicit when Matthew follows this text immediately with the saying, "Whatever you bind on earth will be bound in heaven, and whatever you loose on earth will be loosed in heaven" (Matthew 18:18). So here, too, humans appropriate divine authority, but a new element in Matthew 18:21–22 is evident: forgiveness is unconditional and unlimited.[5]

Jesus' demand to forgive seventy-seven times needs to be seen in its biblical context. In Genesis 4:23–24, we hear Lamech, a descendant of Cain, boast to his wives that he exacted enormous revenge for a minor injury. If Cain was avenged seven times, he says, Lamech will be avenged seventy-seven times. It cannot be mere coincidence that the numbers in the two texts, Genesis and Matthew, are the same. Lamech took seventy-seven-fold revenge, but Jesus calls for seventy-seven-fold forgiveness. Linking the two means that Jesus is calling for the complete renunciation of revenge.[6] A brief look at a concordance to the Bible under "revenge" or "vengeance" reveals an astounding number of occurrences of these words, mainly in the Old Testament. Jesus was going against a powerful tradition, though one can also find strands (especially in the Old Testament Wisdom tradition) that move away from revenge and vengeance.[7]

We see in Jesus' sayings about forgiveness several striking and radical claims: the authority of humans to declare divine forgiveness, the unlimited character of forgiveness, and the renunciation of revenge. While these move well beyond the notion of reciprocal forgiveness found in Jewish tradition around the time of Jesus (e.g., Sirach 28:2), we think they are of a piece with his call to love enemies, especially the renunciation of revenge and the call for unconditional forgiveness.

We are fortunate to have a text in which the early church describes how it would live out Jesus' understanding of forgiveness. Although Matthew 18:15–17 is placed on the lips of Jesus, most scholars think it reflects the practice of the early church.[8] In fact, the use of the word "church" (*ekklesia*) strongly points in that direction, since we have no evidence that Jesus organized specific ecclesial communities.

Here is the text, following the NRSV:

> If another member of the church sins against you, go and point out the fault when the two of you are alone. If the member listens to you, you have regained that one. But if you are not listened to, take one or two others along with you, so that every word may be confirmed by the evidence of two or three witnesses. If the member refuses to listen to them, tell it to the church; and if the offender refuses to listen even to the church, let such a one be to you as a Gentile and a tax collector.

Note first that it is the *victim* who is expected to initiate the process of addressing whatever violation of his person has occurred. This implies several things. First, the community has an understanding that wrongs done by someone to another are to be addressed by the person who is wronged, not by the leader of the community. This thinking is perhaps based on Leviticus 19:17, which calls individuals to reprove their neighbors for wrongs done to them. Also implicit is that the victim is prepared to forgive the offender if the offender apologizes or otherwise makes amends. Placing the responsibility on the victim presumes that the victim is not weak or passive but has the strength to confront the offender, and that the victim is aware of an expectation that he is to do this. The goal is to "regain" the offender, not to exclude him (Matthew 18:15).

The victim is to approach the offender privately, not to bring the complaint to the whole congregation, or gossip about the offender, and thus plant a seed of bitterness in the community. Moreover, doing this privately respects the dignity of the offender and avoids humiliating him in front of others, which would only make him defensive and likely cause the attempted reconciliation to fail. Perhaps the advice in Ephesians 4:26 not to let the sun go down on one's anger is understood here as well: respond quickly to the wrong. This private approach has a further virtue: perhaps the "victim" was, in fact, a victim of his own imagination, and the "offender" had not actually meant to offend him, so this could be cleared up privately.

Should the offender not listen to this private approach, the victim is to take one or two others along to witness the conversation. This means that the victim is less likely later to escalate his complaint (the presumed offender, having heard the initial complaint, could point out that the story had been changed). At the same time, the presence of other community members increases the pressure on the offender, while, however, still keeping the matter largely confidential and minimizing the risk of humiliating him. The text implies that the witnesses are there at least partly to support the victim.[9]

Finally, if the offender does not listen to the victim and a couple of other people, only then is the matter is to be brought to the whole congregation. And the community, assuming that it regards the grievance as valid and the offender as unrepentant, is to shun him henceforth. It is unclear whether we are to understand this as excommunication or as an escalation of pressure on the offender, with the hope that this will result in his apologetic return to the community.[10] In any case, the community is to take responsibility for addressing this grievance, not just ignoring it and hoping it will go away.

This is a psychologically insightful text that provides a picture of forgiveness as a complex process of addressing injury and seeking reconciliation. There is no advice to just "forgive and forget." Wrongs are taken seriously and addressed responsibly. What is at stake is nothing less than the health of the whole community. Even today, congregations could learn much from Jesus' advice. For example, conflicts involving claims of being wronged in some way, or slighted, ignored, or demeaned, would not be allowed to fester and disturb or polarize the congregation. Leaders would not be expected to resolve such issues; the victims and the congregation would be responsible for addressing them. On the other hand, few congregations today would be willing to take the drastic step of excommunicating or shunning the offender. Still, the sensitive procedures called for in this text could be incorporated without the final drastic step. As in Jesus' instructions, the church would give priority to the health and flourishing of the community.

In Mark 12:28–31, Matthew 22:36–38, and Luke 10:25–27, Jesus links two commandments that are not joined in the Old Testament: the commands to love God (Deuteronomy 6:5) and to love the neighbor (Leviticus 19:18). They are to be pursued with equal seriousness. In the parable of the "Good Samaritan," the meaning of "neighbor" gets stretched and then extended beyond any boundary in the command to love enemies. This linkage of love of God and love of neighbor could be said to culminate in the virtual identification of the two that we see in 1 John, where great weight is placed on love of neighbor, without which there is no real love of God. Here, too, interpersonal relationships and community are given special seriousness and prominence.

We believe that the texts on forgiveness attributed to Jesus embody great emotional intelligence and even go beyond most discussions of emotional intelligence. To demonstrate this, we want to explore further the nature of forgiveness and the role that emotional intelligence plays in forgiveness.

The first thing to note is that forgiveness, as we have seen, has to do with repairing relationships, thus restoring the health of the community. The point of having emotional intelligence is also to be able to function effectively in community, creating and maintaining healthy, functional relationships. In fact, that is the purpose of this book—to promote an understanding of emotional intelligence for church leaders and congregations and the necessity of emotional intelligence for nurturing healthy relationships and communities.

The procedure set out for addressing wrongs within the community (Matthew 18:15–17) would require strong emotional intelligence skills. The victim is assigned responsibility for initiating redress of his own grievances. This requires some essential emotional intelligence skills, including self-awareness, assertiveness, and impulse control, as well as optimism that risking confrontation with his victimizer will result in reconciliation or healing. A mechanism is to be put in place to assist the victim in addressing his concerns, but the mechanism will also help to prevent the victim from exploiting his victimhood by exaggerating its seriousness. The mechanism allows the process of addressing grievances to occur largely in confidence, which also prevents the putative victim from being unfairly defamed. Conflict is nipped in the bud before the seed of dissension can be sown in the community. The process shows a keen awareness of the need for social responsibility.

By contrasting Jesus' unlimited forgiveness ("seventy-seven times," Matthew 18:22) with Lamech's unlimited revenge (Genesis 4:24), Jesus effectively abolished revenge for those who would follow him. This also means that lesser expressions of revenge, such as holding grudges or retaliatory demeaning of the other, are also ruled out. In fact, this becomes explicit in Matthew 5:21–22, where anger and especially humiliating and contemptuous expressions are condemned. This would require impulse control and stress tolerance, as well as the self-awareness and empathy to be conscious of the extent to which one's actions represent out-of-control emotions and to be aware of the damage one may have caused. Luke's portrait of Jesus exemplifies in an especially impressive way this renunciation of revenge by refusing to call for retaliation against his tormenters and executioners, even calling upon God to forgive them.[11] Jesus' example, and that of many who have been inspired by Jesus, have themselves inspired us to temper our vindictive tendencies, and they have encouraged and validated forgiveness as a powerful tool for ending the cycle of violence.

In another text, persons are told that if they have anything against their neighbors, they should leave their gifts at the altar and first be reconciled with their brother or sister (Matthew 5:23–24). Here the victim does *not* take the initiative. The members of the community are to have such self-awareness and empathy that they are aware of the impact of their words or actions upon others and urgently seek reconciliation. It is not only victims who are to address their own grievances; all members of the community are to take responsibility for eliminating causes of dissension before they grow and become divisive. They are to assume social responsibility for others in the community. Perhaps this is part of what Jesus had in mind in blessing peacemakers (Matthew 5:9).

Forgiveness can open the door for the future by removing the power of the past with its dead weight, its power to reach into one's future and shape it. As Archbishop Tutu said, "There is no future without forgiveness."[12] This is especially true for the victim, because it is the victim who has the power to forgive. But the victim may be so tortured by the past that she cannot move into the future. The metaphor of "debt" used in Matthew's version of the Lord's Prayer (6:12) is a very apt metaphor. The victim may feel that the perpetrator is in debt to her for restitution, for an apology, or for some other act to recognize the hurt inflicted. To forgive is to cancel that debt, to recognize that it will never be repaid fully or at all, that life is possible without it being repaid, and that one can begin moving into the future. We mentioned the woman whose husband was murdered and who discovered that she had to let go, however hard that was. Such examples show what strong emotional intelligence skills are required to forgive in the sense of letting go of debts, of anger, resentment, and hatred.

Our discussion of the victim operates on the assumption that the victim has overcome a common obstacle: feeling responsible for what happened. Victims may blame themselves. This probably happens mainly when the violation involves acts such as rape, spousal abuse, or fraud. In our culture, victims of such abuse are only too often blamed on their actions or failure to act. Many violations—such as being robbed, being the victim of a medical error, being run into by another automobile—are unlikely to be blamed on the victim or be seen by the victim as his fault. But in cases where it is common to blame the victim, victims will require a measure of emotional intelligence just to accept that they are really victims, to accept their innocence, and thus be in a position to forgive. Unwarranted shame can forestall any possibility of moving toward forgiveness either of the self or of the other.

If the perpetrator feels the need for forgiveness, he is literally at the mercy of the victim. However, totally unexpected acts of forgiveness by the victim (or those who share the victim's suffering, such as the family) can have the potential to shock the perpetrator and reawaken his humanity. If this happens, the cycle of violation and recrimination is even more effectively broken, not only for those most directly involved but also for many who simply hear stories of unexpected forgiveness. The actions of the Amish community in response to the murder of many of their members probably inspired many others, as did the late Nelson Mandela, who forgave those who had kept him in prison for twenty-seven years.

An Internet search shows that stories of people who have forgiven the murder of a son, daughter, or spouse are surprisingly common. In these stories, the victim's family typically must engage in a protracted struggle to reach the point of forgiving the killer. Often it is the religious training of the person that had emphasized the importance of forgiveness that enabled the family member to move toward forgiveness. Very often, when the family member seeks out the murderer and personally offers forgiveness, the murderer is so shocked that he is finally able to accept the enormity of his guilt and begin recovering his humanity. But this act can also be a powerful experience for the family member. Often, she speaks of having a load lifted off her, of finally getting free of bitterness and being able to move on. The story of Mary Johnson of Minneapolis exemplifies these stages of forgiveness. When she sought out in prison and hugged the man who killed her only son, "I felt something leave me. . . . Instantly I knew all the hatred, bitterness and animosity—I knew it was gone."[13] The murderer was also changed. They now live next door to each other.

The power of the parable of the prodigal son lies precisely in the utterly undeserved acceptance by the father of his wayward and ungrateful son. The father's embrace of his returning son is especially shocking because of the lavishness of the celebration of his son's return. Much of the potency of this parable probably lies in the fact that it involves a father and a son, a relationship that is powerful, complex, and can be fraught with tension. The role of the elder son is to express the offense we all feel when ingrates and the disobedient are showered with grace and affection or are simply lucky. In Deuteronomy 21:18–21, the disobedient son is to be killed. In stark contrast, here the disobedient son is welcomed back, although he returns humiliated and expecting at best permission to be a servant in the household. Yet what would better restore the humanity, gratitude, and probably fidelity of the son than this act of unexpected graciousness? We can envision a transformed son, transformed by grace and by forgiveness. The father in the parable is an exemplar of remarkable emotional intelligence. He allowed his joy at the return of his son to give expression to unconditional love unstained or diminished by the years of disappointment and worry.

In the previous chapter we also discussed the redemptive power of love. The text about loving enemies only implied this power, but we tried to show that it had the goal of transforming the enemy, in part by resisting the abusive behavior of the enemy and trying to connect with the humanity of the enemy. Forgiveness helps us understand better the redemptive power of love because of its capacity for healing relationships. For Jesus, forgiveness is grace, the unexpected and undeserved embrace of the other, even the one who hates and abuses us, who does not deserve to be embraced or loved. At a zoo once, we heard the trainer of the zoo's big cats explain how he treats them: he always rewards positive behavior but ignores bad behavior. In a similar way, humans are more likely to be transformed by positive regard than by punishment, reproach, or negative emotions. But to respond to hurt with kindness and love requires emotional intelligence.

Forgiveness is about repairing damaged relationships. But it is a complex phenomenon. It is the act of the victim, because only the victim can forgive. But does forgiving a perpetrator help mainly the victim or the perpetrator? We argue that it is the victim who is the primary benefactor. How so? The trauma of violation, whether physical or psychic, can have a powerful effect on the victim and can stir up anger and the desire for revenge that diminishes the victim's peace of mind and ability to relate to others. It can make one fearful, hateful, bitter, depressed, isolated and, therefore, less able to create and maintain healthy relationships. Forgiveness means the courageous act of letting go of the transgression, which is likely to take an extended period of time. Some researchers distinguish between different levels of forgiveness—the inner level, affecting mainly the victim, and the interpersonal level, which is where relational healing can occur.[14] In other words, forgiveness can benefit the victim whether or not the perpetrator is directly involved. And this benefit can enable the victim to function better and risk establishing healthy relationships once again.

Our view is that violation represents a fundamental assault on a person's dignity and very personhood, an assault on the person's sense of safety, a denial of who they are as persons, and this is why violation is so powerful and hard to leave behind. Memory of violation, of insult, or humiliation can linger a lifetime. That is why forgiveness is so essential: it addresses these fundamental issues of human existence. If forgiveness is the opposite of maintaining grudges,[15] then forgiveness means the relinquishment of grudges, hatred, anger, the right to retaliate or take revenge. There is a sense in which not forgiving leaves the victim in bondage to the perpetrator, because the victim cannot let go of the transgression. Only by letting go of the hurt and anger and resentment of violation can the victim finally break free from her perpetrator. The victim desperately needs the perpetrator to apologize, to show he is truly sorry, perhaps to do something to mend the damage, but these things may never be forthcoming. Forgiveness addresses that desperate need by summoning the courage to let go.

But forgiveness is not simply forgetting, nor does it mean merely overlooking violation and injustice. The state (or other jurisdiction) has its own need to address violation and injury, so forgiving the perpetrator need not mean halting the judicial process or reducing a prison sentence. It just means that the state's needs, not the victim's, are what will be pursued. Moreover, the memory of the violation may be impossible to erase, but forgiving can happen even if the memory remains.

It may take enormous courage for the victim to take the next step and directly address the perpetrator. Simply doing so can be restorative for the victim, because it may give the victim an empowering sense of achievement. It can also free the victim of the burden of bitterness and perhaps of guilt for feeling so bitter and hateful. If the perpetrator is able to truly receive a genuine declaration of forgiveness, both will likely be on their way to healing, though in different ways. For example, the perpetrator may have acted out of his own woundedness, and may experience sufficient transformative acceptance to be able to deal with the destructive effects of his own victimhood. If the perpetrator is dead or not available, forgiveness will still help the victim.

Victims sometimes choose to embrace victimhood and exploit it in various ways. This can be dangerous to the victim as well as to others. They may congratulate themselves on their superior morality, for they did not do such a heinous thing. They may claim they have the right to take revenge in various ways. Victimhood might be used to legitimate anger and hatred. In fact, victims who inhabit their victimhood may become perpetrators. This is true not only on the personal level but also on the societal and national levels, especially if there are leaders who keep reminding people of how they have been victimized in the past in order to excite mass anger, hatred, prejudice, and violence. To forgive is to refuse to embrace victimhood and the many advantages it offers. A perpetrator may later apologize sincerely and ask for forgiveness, but the victim may choose to refuse forgiveness because victimhood allows the victim to hold a club over the perpetrator. Moreover, victims may exaggerate the extent of damage caused by the violation in order to make victimhood even more useful. We believe that Jesus refused to embrace victimhood and called for his followers to do the same. His call to forgive meant exactly that: we refuse to see ourselves as victims even when we are, in fact, victims. Clinging to victimhood may blind us to the humanity of others, to their pain and their struggles. It can destroy empathy and make forgiveness almost impossible. Emotional intelligence includes the refusal to hang on to the advantages of victimhood.

If we ask how the practice of forgiveness might be implemented in the congregation, we have a place to begin: Matthew 18:21–22. We noted that responsibility is placed on the victim to address grievances, which also recognizes a basic fact about forgiveness—namely, that only the victim can truly forgive.[16] But Jesus also placed the onus on all members to be aware of the impact of words and actions that might have hurt others. These texts assume, therefore, that there are *norms* that have been established for community life and that the healthy functioning of the community is a high priority. To implement the practice of forgiveness in congregations today, the same is probably needed: norms for how those who feel hurt should act, norms for how the community should deal with the victims and with the community, and practices to facilitate addressing situations that have the potential to create wider conflict. In addition, there should be norms about the expected sensitivity, empathy, and self-awareness of individuals regardless of whether they have themselves been hurt. The norms establish expectations of "what we do here," how we function as a community. Leaders, of course, have to model these behaviors and work to establish the norms and explain their significance. This is really a task of leading the congregation toward spiritual maturity. It is not just a matter of corporate management; it is of the very essence of what it means to be a follower of Jesus.

We think that congregations and their leaders need to think carefully about the role of public confession and forgiveness. Can that become simply cheap grace? How do public confession and forgiveness aid, or detract from, the practice for forgiveness that Jesus taught and that required a high level of personal and social responsibility?

Consider the role of the leader. Jesus' advice in Matthew 18:21–22 would seem to free the leader from responsibility for personal involvement in addressing conflicts among individuals. If the leader were to follow this pattern, it would mean working to establish and maintain norms that define relationships among members. In many ways, the development of healthy interpersonal skills would help to realize many of the primary goals of Jesus' teaching on loving enemies and forgiveness. If such development does not happen in congregations committed to Jesus, where will it take place? Engagement in civil society is likely to help, but in most cases, civil groups have a different function—namely, to achieve certain specific goals that may or may not include the intentional development of interpersonal relational skills. Congregations could contribute a great deal to civil society by being communities where healthy interpersonal skills—emotional intelligence!—are being learned and practiced.

Forgiveness needs to be an intentional focus of the entire congregation—a subject addressed in sermons and in adult education, explored with appropriate resources in Sunday school, incorporated into staff relationships, and much more. A good help in thinking about how to do this is the article on "The Church as Forgiving Community" by University of Wisconsin forgiveness researchers Chad Magnuson and Robert Enright.[17] The have created a model called "The Forgiving Communities" (family, school, and church). It is based on Enright's four stages of forgiveness: (1) uncovering anger—acknowledging the pain and exploring the injustice; (2) deciding to forgive—exploring forgiveness and making a commitment to work toward forgiveness; (3) working on forgiveness—reframing and developing empathy and compassion for the offender and bearing the pain; and (4) the outcome—experiencing the healing. Magnuson and Enright have already tested this in schools in Belfast, Ireland, and Milwaukee, with promising results. They focus especially on children. For congregations, their proposed model "consists of multiple levels of forgiveness education that take place at fixed times each year to cultivate a culture of forgiveness and the expectation that forgiveness is part of the congregation's existence not only for a short period of time, but for life."[18] Although forgiveness education needs to happen at multiple levels in the congregation (they discuss each one), "the pastor . . . is the prime target in the forgiveness education program and in developing the Church as Forgiving Community."[19]

Forgiveness, we have argued, is deeply rooted in Christian tradition and in the teaching of Jesus. It is a treasure embodying profound insight into human relationships and into healthy communities. However, it has played a relatively minor role in the literature of emotional intelligence, even though it has been quite extensively studied by social scientists and psychologists.[20] These studies have demonstrated the power and necessity of forgiveness and thus also the wisdom of the teaching of Jesus. It is our hope that congregations in the future will focus more intentionally on forgiveness and on cultivating a culture of forgiveness. Not only would that lead to healthier congregations, it would also be an important contribution to civic life in the communities that they serve.

TEN

The Emotionally Intelligent Congregation

Emotional intelligence is not a static characteristic within humans; the same is true for congregations. It is developed through an ongoing process that builds upon a history of meaningful relationships between pastors and the congregation, plus deep interpersonal relationships that congregants have with each other. The congregation's identity as a place of healing and personal support is no accident. It will have been guided by strong leaders, both clergy and lay, who sense the importance of being emotionally intelligent, even if they do not use that term.

The emotionally intelligent congregation is a community of people within which a good number of basic human needs are met. Some philosophers say we cannot be human alone. There is growing awareness of the devastating psychological effects that extended solitary confinement has on prison inmates. It drives some people insane. Relationships are central to our growth as individuals. Research also confirms the positive relationship between high-quality interpersonal relationships and physical health. Positive human contact can lengthen our life dramatically. In their book *Primal Leadership*, Daniel Goleman, Richard Boyatzis, and Annie McKee say:

Research in intensive care units has shown that the comforting presence of another person not only lowers the patient's blood pressure, but also slows the secretion of fatty acids that block arteries. More dramatically, whereas three or more incidents of intense stress within a year (say, serious financial trouble, being fired, or divorced) triple the death rate in socially isolated middle aged men, they have *no impact* whatsoever on the death rate of men who have cultivated many positive, close relationships.[1]

Cutting off a person from his or her community can have devastating consequences. Seventy years ago, anthropologist Walter Cannon discussed the practice of "bone pointing" within Australian aboriginal tribes.[2] Tribal members understood that having a bone pointed at you by the community's shaman meant that you no longer existed. You stopped being real. In one instance cited, a bone was simply pointed at an individual during a ritual conducted by the community's shaman. The results were dramatic. The person trembled, fell backward as in a swoon, and writhed, moaning. After composing himself, the previously healthy person retreated to his hut and refused to eat. Within a short time, he was dead. Cannon, citing William James's work in *Principles of Psychology* (1905) on the extreme effects of total social isolation, maintains that within such a primitive tribe, that specific community was the whole world to an individual. A person had nowhere else to go where he would be considered a real human being again. That kind of enclosed culture is quite different from life as we experience it. Most of us are considered real within many different communities; hence we experience many different ways we can remain alive. Even just going to a bar to have a drink affirms that we are a real human being.

Communal acceptance remains one of the gifts congregations can offer people. Walk into many congregations, and you are likely to find people ready to talk to you.[3] Many individuals have jobs that bounce them around the country every few years. Sage advice to these people is to identify a congregation that is compatible with their belief systems and become an active member. Showing up regularly at coffee hour or an adult forum gives a stranger a way to become known by others, possibly on a first-name basis. Within six months of beginning to participate in a congregation, a new member will likely be asked to serve on a committee or engage in some group activity. Once accepted as a regular attender, if not a member, the individual would likely receive a visit from someone in the congregation should he or she be suddenly hospitalized.

Even apart from times of crisis, people's connection with a congregation can provide the community they need to make it through the following week. Some people with mental illness get enough human contact, enough support and encouraging words, to last them that long. For some elderly people, shaking hands with the minister on the way out of the service is the only human touch they receive for weeks on end. In short, the human contact people receive from their congregations can make a huge difference in many people's lives. An emotionally intelligent congregation understands this deeply and ensures that its emotional climate remains positive. Remaining a welcoming community may take ongoing work, but EQ congregations know the importance of their members continuing to reach out to visitors.

Recently, many mainline congregations have been concerned that few young adults, ages twenty-one to forty, attend worship services anymore. Congregational leaders may not realize what a significant resource they offer their community—namely, a place where people can connect with others in warm and supportive relationships. People may not feel a need for corporate worship, but they may be looking for a way to connect in smaller face-to-face groups. Congregations can provide such a resource more easily and quickly than other organizations in our culture, even reaching a younger generation.

Congregations in western North Dakota are responding to this need to connect. With the discovery of oil in the area, thousands of workers have come to the state for the employment it offers, but not enough housing is available in communities close to the wells. Some workers commute long distances between home and work. Others simply rent rooms in towns near their work and return home to family and friends as their work schedule allows. Congregations in the area have found ways to help these workers enjoy positive human contact, some hosting Sunday afternoon dinners or evening coffee houses, a clear alternative to bars and brothels.

Genuine community—human bonding—is based on trust. A sort of chicken-and-egg phenomenon occurs here: community is based on trust, but the experience of community also engenders trust. The importance of human bonding has been emphasized and given a scientific basis by recent research into the neuropeptide oxytocin. The roles of oxytocin in human lactation (the milk "letdown") and in bonding mother to infant, as well as in childbirth, have been known for some time. Because of these roles, the chemical was thought for some time to be peculiar to females, but it has been shown to play important roles in both females and males.

Studies in the past decade have shown that when humans are in close, friendly contact, oxytocin is released, and this generates empathy, trust, and pleasure, which strengthen the bonding relationship. Small amounts of oxytocin are released each time we receive a hug from a good friend. Apparently we should receive a few hugs a day to maintain a positive, buoyant spirit. Researchers who introduced oxytocin into subjects' nasal passages found "a substantial increase in trust among humans."[4] Another group of researchers reported, "We find that subjects in the oxytocin group show no change in their trusting behavior after they learned that their trust had been breached several times while subjects receiving a placebo decrease their trust."[5]

Many aspects of congregational life can and do produce oxytocin. When a congregation stands to sing one of its favorite hymns, we can sense the trust and the feeling of unity it engenders. Being part of a congregation's liturgy and rituals has the capacity to create peace of mind and a sense of rootedness, if only for a short period of time. For many people, the passing of the peace before communion and then coming forward to receive communion produces a similar feeling of safety and belonging. The coffee hour following worship may entail superficial conversation, but for many it provides a way to reconnect and remain current with the lives of others. When the quality of the coffee is good and there are snacks for the kids, this experience of fellowship can spark deeper engagements with others—as if oxytocin were served along with something to drink. For members experiencing a setback in personal relationships or a crushing event at their place of employment, a phone call from someone in the congregation who simply listens, and perhaps offers a prayer, can provide a perspective on life that saves them from despair. When facing a serious operation the next day, a visit from someone in the congregation who holds our hand while offering a prayer can make us feel cared for and at peace about that operation. A time of team building before a meeting that begins with everyone in the circle sharing briefly what is transpiring in their life also can promote this kind of trust and belonging.

Six Marks of an Emotionally Intelligent Congregation

We have identified six ways a congregation can promote emotionally intelligent behavior. Each of these marks helps people within a congregation stay connected in positive ways. An emotionally intelligent congregation:

1. keeps the three components of congregational life alive and healthy—climate, theology, and vision;
2. develops an immune system that enables church leaders and members to intervene when toxic interchanges threaten to disrupt a positive community experience;
3. ensures that congregational norms—the unconscious, unwritten rules about the way people are to behave—are made conscious and possibly altered to remain positive and relationship enhancing;
4. expects decision-making or study groups to engage in some type of team building before they begin their work and to conclude with some type of evaluation of group process before people leave;
5. sponsors small-group ministries where people can connect in meaningful ways; and
6. ensures that members and constituents receive prompt and effective pastoral care.

An Emotionally Intelligent Congregation Keeps the Three Components of Congregational Life Alive and Healthy— Climate, Theology, and Vision

Congregational life can be described using three interlocking circles, as shown in figure 10.1. Each of these circles will have advocates in the congregation who will say, "This one is the most important of the three." The vision people are convinced that a great strategic plan will solve most of the congregation's problems. Other members assert that more Bible study and theological discussion will bring members closer together. The climate people claim that if leaders can help everyone in the congregation feel good about each other, the congregation will thrive.

While all three are indeed important to congregational health, climate is the most important. Without a positive relational climate within a congregation, a superior theology or dynamic vision will produce few results. Once members of a congregation create a warm, supportive, and caring climate, however, they can effectively develop a common understanding of who they are as Christians and embrace an exciting vision of where they ought to go next. When important decisions need to be made, consideration is always given to how these decisions affect the congregation's climate. When possible, these decisions are altered to sustain or increase the good feelings members have about their congregation.

FIGURE 10.1. Three Arenas of Congregational Life

An Emotionally Intelligent Congregation Develops an Immune System That Enables Church Leaders and Members to Intervene When Toxic Interchanges Threaten to Disrupt a Positive Community Experience

Our bodies contain incredible immune systems. When germs or viruses invade our bodies, this system springs into action. Foreign entities are contained and are flushed out of the system. In a similar way, an EQ congregation has an immune system that addresses and contains toxic interchanges of its members or outside threats to its health. It begins when the governing board is as concerned about the emotional life of the congregation as the state of their physical plant or a balanced budget. It is clear to them that a positive congregational climate is as important as being in a financially healthy state. When there is a complaint about the pastor, the board has an active pastor/parish relations committee that springs into action. (We say more about this in the chapter on the EQ pastor.) When there is a heated interchange between two members on a board or committee and it remains unresolved, some informal phone calls are made by the pastor or other church leaders who move to resolve this conflict in a positive manner—not that conflict in the congregation is bad, but some conflicts have a nasty quality to them where people's integrity is impugned. When certain members engage in triangulation (which occurs when Person A and Person B bond over their concern for Person C), they are called on this behavior. Congregants are also called on the practice of gossip that demeans other members. In addition, the EQ congregation seeks out and calls a pastor known for his or her emotional intelligence skills who is skilled in developing and maintaining a healthy emotional climate within a congregation. These are just some examples of an immune system that keeps a congregation engaged in emotionally intelligent interchanges between people.

The apostle Paul, who had a systemic understanding of the church, talked about the body of Christ as being made up of numerous parts but functioning as a single organism. Paul makes frequent mention of infections that threaten the health of the body. He mentions grumblers, malcontents, people who "bite and devour one another" (Galatians 5:15), and groups unbending in their contentiousness (Jude 1:4). He warns against people who are fractious and quarreling, jealous, angry, selfish, slandering, gossiping, and conceited (2 Corinthians 12:19–20). All of these may be considered viruses that can invade a church system.

Viral infection and relational conflict function in similar ways. A host cell (in a congregation, group, or individual) does not tolerate the virus's invasive behavior. In other words, conflict between members is not left to fester and expand. When people involved in the conflict are allowed to malign "those others"—their opponents in the conflict, or *any* other people—soon that conflict will escalate, and more people will become entangled in these disagreements. When a congregation does not have an active immune system to counteract this process, the level of conflict rises to the point that members are no longer dealing with a disagreement but become locked into warring factions.

Four viruses can be especially harmful to the body of a congregation. Peter Steinke, in his book *Healthy Congregations*, identifies these as secrets (negative information about others that remains hidden), accusations (faultfinding), lies (clear deceptions), and triangulation.[6] The presence of secrets, accusations, lies, or triangles is not itself the disease. Rather, these enable the disease process. When a congregational disagreement rises to the level of a contest, people start to fight "dirty." They begin to spread malicious information about their opposition (secrets, lies). Their major objective now is not to resolve differences but to come out looking good. Personal attacks increase and replace any attempt to identify problems. As the conflict continues to escalate, the major objective of each side is to hurt, weaken, punish, or humiliate the other.

Triangulation occurs when person A becomes anxious about the words and behavior of person C and engages person B in a conversation about C. The dysfunctionality of the relationship between person A and person C becomes a secret between persons A and B. Triangulation requires person B to buy into this secret, and it can devastate the life of person C when it involves false accusations. When persons A and B continue to be anxious about person C, they may try to persuade other people in the congregation that person C is a problem.

Sometimes person C is the pastor of the congregation, and it is here that an active pastor/parish relations committee can be of enormous help. Members of an effective committee can talk with persons A and B and ascertain which complaints about the pastor are on target and should be addressed with the pastor and which concerns are not accurate and should be challenged. This process also brings issues into the open, which allows the pastor (person C) to work on his relationship with persons A and B.

It is not unusual for a member (person A) to attempt to form a triangle with the pastor, asking him to be an ally (person B) against person C. If the congregation's immune system is healthy, the pastor refuses to be engaged in such a triangle and invites person A to talk directly to person C. The congregation's immune system is strengthened even further when other members refuse to be engaged in any triangle and encourage direct conversation between members. Another element of a healthy congregational immune system is a specific board policy that anonymous feedback, such as a letter of complaint about the pastor or some aspect of congregational life, will not be taken seriously. Such a congregation may find a pastor, during the announcement time of a service, saying, "Hey folks, last week we received an anonymous letter from a congregant complaining about some aspect of our congregational life. You need to know we threw it into the garbage before reading it. In this congregation we do not take seriously anonymous feedback from members. We need to grow up spiritually and learn to address our differences face-to-face." The board encourages other groups in the congregation to follow a similar process.

When viewed from this perspective, an emotionally intelligent congregation is one that has learned to manage toxic interchanges when they first arise. Congregational leaders have an intuitive sense of how to nip these potential conflicts in the bud. These interventions can range from making a simple phone call to calm someone down after a meeting, to calling together people engaged in a dispute to have them talk through their differences directly with each other.

In the next chapter on the EQ pastor, we explore some of the skills clergy can acquire to support an active immune system. A pastor can also be instrumental in identifying the congregational members who possess good emotional intelligence skills and who can step in and address behavior fueled by excessive anxiety and conflict.

An Emotionally Intelligent Congregation Ensures That Congregational Norms—the Unconscious, Unwritten Rules about the Way People Are to Behave—Are Made Conscious and Possibly Altered to Remain Positive and Relationship Enhancing

All of us are guided by the norms of the specific communities to which we belong. For the most part, this guidance system functions at an unconscious level. Members of the congregation are likely to punish people when their norms are violated. They may simply let fly with a caustic remark when a norm has been violated, which may leave the violator confused, or they may really dress down the person.

When we enter a new community, we might unwittingly violate its norms, because we unconsciously abide by the norms of another community we belonged to. For example, a young family might bring their three-year-old daughter into worship with them and, rather than trying to keep the child quiet, allow her to talk out loud and walk up and down the aisle. They do not realize her behavior is not acceptable in this particular congregation, because they come from a congregation that is okay with that behavior.

Emotionally intelligent congregations periodically (once every three to five years) conduct an event to raise their norms into consciousness to ensure that congregants' behaviors are congruent with how they see themselves functioning. Roy's book *Discerning Your Congregation's Future* details such a process.[7] He suggests members enjoy a meal together and then spend ninety minutes reflecting on norms. Aspects of congregational life are identified, and small groups—each group focusing on an assigned dimension of congregational life—take thirty minutes to come up with all the unwritten rules the congregation has in that specific area of life.

Groups might explore norms about children, men and women, conflict or how we disagree with one another, money, use of the building, expectations of members, the role of ushers, treatment of clergy and staff, who is welcome here, and conduct in worship. Small groups write their observations on newsprint and then share these with the large group.

For example, a group that works on the norms related to children may have on its list:

- Children are allowed to gather around the font at a baptism.
- We prize having children in our congregation, and we work to make them feel welcome.
- We get upset when children are left free to run in the hallways.
- When children misbehave and are not disciplined by a caregiver, we get angry with the caregiver.
- When children are noisy in our formal, traditional service, we feel free to turn around and glare at them, reminding parents that child-care services are available.
- Children are not allowed to be in the church kitchen by themselves.

Once all groups have reported their findings, the group as a whole can reflect on norms that have a bite to them—that are negative and should be changed. If, for example, the group working on norms for children had come in with the observations listed above, those present could be asked, "If you were a parent with a young child and these were the norms, would you feel welcome here?" If the answer is no, then an EQ congregation will work to change the way members behave when children are around.

Identifying norms within a congregation is not easy work. Those who attempt to pinpoint a congregation's real norms may feel like they are confessing congregational sins. In many ways, a congregation is saying to itself, "We would like to believe we are some kind of special community of faith, but this is how we actually behave."

Norms are not easy to change. They require hard, intentional work. In some cases, a behavioral covenant needs to be written and signed by members. The goal is to change behavior. In a congregation with average worship of two hundred, not everyone will sign such a covenant, but if a majority do, behavior will change. If, for example, the group that dealt with the unwritten rules about conflict and how members disagree with one another decided that people primarily dealt with conflict by gossiping, a behavioral covenant would look something like this: "With my signature, I covenant to refrain from participating in any conversation in which another member of the congregation is referred to in a negative way. In other words, when someone comes up to me and begins talking negatively about someone else in the congregation, I promise I will say to her, 'I'm sorry. I cannot participate in this type of conversation. If you have something against this other person, you need to go talk with her directly. I will even go with you as you confront this person directly.'" When enough people sign such a behavioral covenant, this negative behavior will soon grind to a halt.

Or if a congregation discovers that its members are friendly to each other but not to strangers, members could write a behavioral covenant like this: "I promise that as soon as the worship service is over, I will first try to find someone I don't know or don't know well, and I will introduce myself to them and engage them in conversation. Only after this will I go talk with my friends." Even when only a minority of congregational members signs this covenant, it will have a dramatic effect on what visitors experience when attending for the first time.

A congregation might also be able to bring about a change in norms without asking members to sign a covenant. In one congregation that for decades had consistently given visitors a cold shoulder, a few leaders informally decided to behave differently. They simply agreed among themselves to talk after worship with one person they did not know before visiting with their friends. Occasionally, they commented to other members that they were meeting interesting people this way, suggested others try it, and answered their questions about how to deal with awkward moments, such as the discovery that the person they greeted had been a member for ten years. Talking first with a newcomer gradually became "the way we do things," and more than twenty years after the initial efforts to change the congregation's culture, visitors still frequently comment that they have not been as warmly received in any other congregation they have visited.

An Emotionally Intelligent Congregation Expects Decision-Making or Study Groups to Engage in Some Type of Team Building Before They Begin Their Work and to Conclude with Some Type of Evaluation of Group Process Before People Leave

Before beginning their tasks, groups in the church need to become teams, so team-building activities are valuable tools. Team building can be done many ways. Individuals might be asked to share something personal about themselves before engaging the agenda of the meeting. A group leader might say, "Let's all take a few minutes to share the high and low points of our week." Or she might ask, "Where did we experience the grace of God this week, or where did we observe something demonic?" Everybody in that meeting is given a turn to respond. This exchange may take only ten to fifteen minutes—at times thirty minutes—but it makes all the difference in the world as the group begins its task.

The quality of decision-making is always higher when a group first engages in some type of team building. That makes sense. We usually trust people more when we learn something new and positive about them. When people trust one another, they are much more likely to voice an opinion that is somewhat controversial, which leads to a more effective decision-making process.

At times the lack of team building at the beginning of a gathering can imperil its process. For example, when a group dives right into its agenda, a group member may have to remain silent about a tragedy she just experienced. Perhaps a family member died recently, or someone close to her was involved in a bad car accident. For her to function well in this group, she may first need to talk about what happened, in part so she can set it aside for a time. In addition, others in the group can respond with care and support. The group may decide immediately to offer a prayer for this individual. All of this conversation can come under the rubric of "team building."

Equally important is the norm that no meeting ends in the congregation before the group takes a few minutes to evaluate how well they think they worked together. This gives group members time to reflect on their process. They critique not only the decisions that were made but also the way in which those decisions were made. The long-term result of such a practice is that meetings usually become shorter and member satisfaction with their meeting time increases. When the way meetings are conducted within a congregation is mainly dysfunctional and negative, members will continue to find ways to miss meetings or they will refuse to be appointed to serve in decision-making groups.

For example, reflecting on a meeting's process, one member may find the courage to say, "I was really frustrated that we spent about forty minutes talking about something irrelevant to our meeting agenda. We're not using our time well when we try to solve problems that don't belong to our committee." The person chairing the meeting may say internally, "Ouch, that reflects on my leadership of this meeting. Yes, I did allow the meeting to get out of control at that point, and I'm not going to allow that to happen at future meetings." Evaluating a meeting's process before leaving the building has the effect of training the chair or group facilitator how to conduct more efficient meetings as well as teaching team members how to work together more effectively. It just make EQ sense that satisfaction with meetings will increase when congregational groups work together more effectively.

An Emotionally Intelligent Congregation Sponsors Small-Group Ministries Where People Can Connect in Meaningful Ways

One of the goals of a congregation should be for members to experience the support, affirmation, and bonding that come from genuine community. Within deep community, members feel free to share authentic emotional expressions and experience such authenticity from others. In pseudocommunity, members feign authenticity and pretend to be what they are not. Many people have never experienced genuine community. An emotionally intelligent congregation strives to make such an experience of community available to its members by establishing long-term, well-led small groups. The spiritual content of these small groups may vary, from extended Bible studies, theological discussions, and social action/social justice efforts to prayer groups. Regardless of the subject these small groups (ranging from six to twelve participants) address, they need to covenant to stay together for a specific number of meetings or a specific period of time. Some groups gather for extended periods of times, but the makeup of the group continues to change, so it's like starting over every meeting. An example might be a group that meets six weeks on a Lenten Bible study. The group covenants to stay together for those six sessions, so no one can join the group during that period of time. This will allow the opportunity for that group to experience genuine community—marked by the stages of group development described below.

Scott Peck, in his book *The Different Drum*, helps us detail the difference between pseudocommunity and community.[8] Peck's work is from the mid-1980s, but we continue to come back to his outline because he describes this process best. The fact that researchers continue to study and write about small-group development indicates that this process is important to understand. Unfortunately, many congregational leaders are not aware of small-group development theory, and only the exceptional congregation commits to providing its members with high-quality group experiences. When people have experienced this kind of support and depth in a congregation's small group, however, they will wonder how they could live without it.

PSEUDOCOMMUNITY

Peck spent over a year traveling around the country, observing the steps a group of people needs to take to move from pseudocommunity to true community. Pseudocommunity is characterized by members' efforts to be polite to one another. In this stage, we withhold the truth about ourselves from one another. We avoid conflicts and deny our individual differences with others. People speak in generalities. To understand this type of community, we need only to think about the coffee hour following Sunday worship. We are pleasant to one another. We actually enjoy just touching the surface with others. This is not a time when we bring up differences we have with specific members. Nor is it a time to get into deep personal issues with others. If we do need to make significant contact with another member, we may touch base in this setting and agree to meet at another time to pursue it.

CHAOS

The move to greater depth involves members becoming open and honest with one another. When these individual differences begin to surface, the group feels like it is in chaos. Members decide to become honest about what they are really feeling and thinking—they stop withholding the truth about what they perceive is going on in the group. They may openly try to convert other people to their own way of seeing things, to correct them, or to fix or heal them. It is here that differences in biblical understanding, theology, personal/spiritual discipline, and political views begin to appear. In this stage, some members try to control others. They readily engage in a struggle to have their views heard and acknowledged. For people who are conflict averse, the group will feel like it is falling apart.

Many people deny Scott Peck's claim that even when a small group is a support group and not a decision-making group, it will not reach true community unless it goes through this stage. Some church people will always believe that we need to be "Christian" with one another, which to them means being polite and nice to each other. "Can't we just continue to be pleasant with one another and gradually move into true community?" they will ask. The answer is a strong no. When individual differences are not surfaced and acknowledged, the group is going to stay in safe pseudo-community mode. If some group members succeed in getting the group to calm down and move back to being nice—but not truly honest—with one another, the move to depth is truncated. Knowing chaos is a necessary step toward group maturity and productivity allows us to celebrate this stage rather than being in despair about it.

EMPTINESS

This third stage of group development is a bridge between chaos and community. It can also be characterized as a type of "letting go." Group members begin letting go of their expectations and preconceptions of how the group needs to function. People begin to discard their rigid thinking and become more open to hearing how other people think and feel. Individual prejudices begin to become more apparent. People begin to realize that they themselves might need to change.

Slowly group members can begin to acknowledge and appreciate interpersonal differences. People perk up and begin to become interested in the real people who are showing up. They see a side of some people that they hadn't seen before. The rich tapestry of the group begins to take shape, and a deeper appreciation of the group begins to take hold. This is not possible until participants have let go of their perspectives on what others ought to believe and how group members ought to behave.

COMMUNITY

When this fourth stage begins to appear, a new spirit of peace begins to surface. Sadness and grief are still part of the group experience. Group members are aware of what they as individuals and the group as a whole have lost in this struggle, and they are also aware of the cost of getting to this new place. Normally, everyone in the group has had to sacrifice something, but laughter and joy begin to break through. The group experiences a new kind of inclusiveness. Members are aware of their journey to this stage, and they do not want to return to a former pseudocommunity. They begin to talk about their group with a new sense of pride.

Some groups need to end, perhaps because an agreed-upon term has ended. Group members will want to join in a ritual of conclusion as they prepare to part. The bonds that people in such a group have felt need to be acknowledged and celebrated. Rituals have the capacity to express things that go deeper than words. Experiencing genuine community in life is rare, and we need to celebrate it when we come to realize how life giving such a community can be.

A variety of EQ skills will be required for a congregation to establish meaningful groups for members. Besides self-awareness, the traits of empathy, flexibility, and self-control are needed for real community to form. Group members also need to practice forgiveness and love for those who strongly oppose them (their enemies). Even in the midst of the chaos stage, the capacity for optimism, as well as skills in conflict management, need to be present.

We have to realize that true community will rarely be achieved by an entire congregation. Yet it is possible within smaller groups in a congregation, and the emotionally intelligent congregation offers opportunities for such experiences. Some congregations choose to move from being a program-centered congregation to a small-group-oriented one just so more members can experience this kind of community. For a small group to develop depth, however, continuity is necessary, as is a group leader who understands this process and can help a group hang together as it proceeds. Emotionally intelligent congregations realize what in-depth group experiences require, so they select small-group leaders carefully and offer them training to prepare them for the ride.

An Emotionally Intelligent Congregation Ensures That Members and Constituents Receive Prompt and Effective Pastoral Care

We have already mentioned that personal support extends people's lives, allows them to face adversity more effectively, and contributes to overall happiness. When congregants experience a personal crisis, they typically expect that someone from the congregation will come see them, and those who receive a visit from someone who cares about them are going to feel supported. Homebound persons who are called on by the pastor or lay caregiver every two to four weeks are more likely to feel like a part of congregational life than those who receive a personal visit from the pastor only twice a year. High-quality pastoral care can also be seen as an outreach tool. Members on the outer fringes of the congregation will be drawn more deeply into congregational life when someone attends to them when they are in crisis. Providing timely, effective pastoral care will shape the identity of the congregation as a deeply caring community, enhance members' health, and make the congregation much more appealing to visitors and outsiders.

Pastors are usually responsive when members are hospitalized, and some clergy are attentive to homebound members. Some congregations, however, are locked into the notion that only professionally trained clergy are able to provide pastoral care to members. They think the pastor alone is responsible for visiting people who are ill or homebound and do not get involved themselves, which limits the amount of pastoral care that can be offered within a congregation. In addition, congregational leaders may decide that the congregation cannot afford to hire additional staff and on that basis expect their clergyperson to do it all. When the pastoral care needs of members exceed what clergy can offer, often only members dealing with extreme crises are attended to, and pastoral visits are frequently rushed. The opportunities for members to receive personal attention from within the congregation are missed, and members may conclude their congregation is an uncaring place.

From a theological perspective, we recognize that we do not pay someone to do our loving and caring for us. Within the body of Christ, brothers and sisters care for each other. Not everyone is good at pastoral care, however, so emotionally intelligent congregations identify members with gifts for this kind of ministry—those who are good at listening to people, able to empathize with them, and comfortable being in prayer with them. Often, these congregations offer training programs for people who feel called to this ministry, which these members relish. They also offer ongoing supervision for pastoral care team members, so care providers have a chance to review their experiences with others and grow in their skills. This group is seen as part of the pastoral care team for the congregation, and this ministry will contribute to the quality of compassion experienced by members. Such teams can also reach out to nonmembers who are going through some type of personal crisis and who are not members of or receiving care from another congregation. This is where pastoral care becomes a tool of congregational outreach.

Most congregations offer some form of pastoral care. The question is whether pastoral care offered to members is abundant or a scarce commodity. We contend that emotionally intelligent congregations offer members more rather than less pastoral care. It is one concrete way congregants can become "members one of another."

Conclusion

We end where we began—namely, by asserting that congregational health and wholeness is all about relationships. When we remain focused on this, communities of faith will enhance the well-being of all their members. We believe that being a member of an emotionally intelligent congregation is one of the easiest and most effective ways of experiencing genuine community and safeguarding against isolation and loneliness. We believe it is an antidote to the trend in North America of more people living alone and becoming disconnected from others, with devastating effects on their personal health. This trend is documented in the book *Bowling Alone*.[9]

We also believe that emotionally intelligent congregations will address the social ills of our time, reaching out to marginalized people in our society. Such congregations are voices for justice for individuals who are segregated and discriminated against. It is hard to imagine a congregation that consistently demonstrates emotional intelligent behavior internally but does not concern itself with the poor treatment of some citizens or noncitizens of our country. Congregations can model how we are to live together as a country that is becoming, we hope, more emotionally intelligent. All this will lead to an emotionally intelligent human community sharing space on this fragile planet, one where compassion, peace, and justice are possible.

ELEVEN

The Emotionally Intelligent Pastor

Pastoral ministry is all about relationships. You may be a brilliant theologian, excellent at biblical exegesis, an outstanding preacher, a great pastoral care provider, and even give your body to be burned (remember 1 Corinthians 13), but if you are not emotionally intelligent, your ministry as a parish pastor will be difficult. When a pastor has trouble connecting in significant ways with congregants, it puts into question the other skills and abilities he brings to congregational ministry. EQ skills are central to the development of trust within a congregation. Effective ministry relies on trust, and trust is a necessary foundation for other gifts and abilities to be utilized.

Emotional intelligence involves a set of competencies that are not taught in seminary but that are central to pastoral effectiveness. It has to do with character and how we personally express ourselves—how we embody the message we bear. Who we are as a person is as important as what we know and what we do. This does not mean a seminary education is unimportant. It is also essential to pastoral excellence. When a student does not possess adequate emotional intelligence, however, most seminaries do not know how to address this challenge. Those who train clergy need to create an environment within which relationships are the focus and where behavior is critiqued, where people are offered feedback on the impact their words and behavior have on others. People who are already serving congregations or who are studying in seminaries that do not attend to emotional intelligence, however, are not out of luck. At the end of this chapter, we outline ten strategies clergy can use to increase their EQ. But first, how do emotionally intelligent pastors behave? What traits and skills do they possess?

The Involuntary Termination of Clergy

While working with the Alban Institute as a senior consultant, Speed Leas led a research project on the involuntary termination of clergy.[1] When sexual malfeasance was taken out of the scenarios, the lack of skill in managing interpersonal relationships was the number-one reason clergy got fired. As capable as these clergy may have been in other dimensions of congregational life, it was their inability to connect personally with congregants at an emotional level that did them in.

Best Bosses/Worst Bosses

At EQ-HR weeklong workshops, we sometimes ask participants to identify the worst boss they have ever had as well as the best boss. The characteristics of these bosses are similar to those of pastors who exhibit primarily negative and positive emotions, respectively. These are some of participants' descriptions of their worst boss:

- Micromanager
- Has wide mood swings
- Inconsistent
- Doesn't listen
- Is not interested in my personal development
- Gets defensive when challenged
- Loses temper frequently and unpredictably
- It is his way or the highway
- Does not cover my back
- Is a conflict avoider
- Never finds a way to compliment me
- Takes personal credit for everything
- Plays favorites
- Easily irritated
- Is insecure in one-on-one relationships

As you review this list, you can easily identify how these bosses lack emotional intelligence. They do not have the foresight to realize the emotional consequences of their behavior and the impact it has on those around them. The boss who tries to micromanage everyone in his system is unaware of how insulting and demeaning this can be to workers. The boss whose temper flares up frequently and at unpredictable times is out of touch with how she has the whole company on edge most of the time. The boss who gets defensive when challenged will not, over the long haul, get the feedback he needs in order to become a more effective leader. The boss who is a conflict avoider usually has tension bubbling up in all corners of the company's life as conflicts rarely surface and are dealt with. Bosses and pastors who lack emotional intelligence will have many of these negative traits that undermine their credibility. More important, with these characteristics, the trust level in the system will be low, resulting in cynicism and a withholding of the truth telling that makes for effective decisions.

Middle judicatory executives claim they have clergy who exhibit many of these characteristics and that these clergy are struggling to gain respect from their congregants. Clergy exhibiting mainly negative emotions tend to drive people away. Few members will volunteer for congregational roles, and few people outside the congregation will want to join.

What follows are some of the characteristics participants see in "best bosses." These are the traits we would see emotionally intelligent clergy possessing:

- Has a sense of humor and is willing to laugh at herself
- Willing to admit her mistakes
- Has an interest in my personal and professional development
- Takes time to listen to me
- Is open to feedback
- Goes to bat for me
- Offers constructive feedback
- Is usually upbeat and optimistic
- Exhibits self-confidence but is humble about gifts
- Elicits trust by the way he functions
- Draws out the best in me
- Tries to understand what I am experiencing personally
- Calls people on irresponsible behavior, and offers a better way of functioning
- Wins people over by her authenticity
- Able to bring about resolution when conflict occurs

According to judicatory executives, clergy who are sought after by other congregations are those with traits like those on the best-boss list.

What stands out in this second list is an authenticity that people crave. Here is a boss who is open to feedback and willing to admit his mistakes. In addition, this is someone who elicits trust by the way he functions. He has a sense of humor and is able to laugh at himself. He exhibits self-confidence but is also humble about himself. Yet this is also a boss who calls people on irresponsible behavior. She is one who surfaces conflict when it arises and leads people involved into some type of resolution. Likewise, clergy with skills in eliciting positive emotional reactions in people are like magnets. People tend to gravitate toward them. As a result, they are usually surrounded by members who volunteer to work with them. They are able to attract talented people to fill important congregational roles. In addition, they have the capacity to attract outsiders to the congregation.

Observe carefully what is not on the best-boss list. No one mentioned how brilliant they were or their outstanding leadership ability. Being a great orator or being an organizational genius was not mentioned, either. Most traits had to do with their personal relationships with their employees.

Core Characteristics of Effective Pastors

At the core of whatever spiritual guidance a pastor offers a congregation needs to be a self-aware person who has the capacity to connect in meaningful ways with people—all kinds of people. Self-awareness is seen by experts as the cornerstone of emotional intelligence. When we are unaware of our emotions, we will not be able to manage them.

Managing one's emotions is no easy task. Emotions are not self-generated or consciously produced. They hit us like a body blow, similar to turning and physically running into another person. Our emotional intelligence is determined by how we manage these unbidden emotions. Self-awareness puts us in touch with these emotions along with their intensity. Feelings are the labels we place on these emotions. Our growth in emotional intelligence has to do with our capacity to plumb the depths of these emotions, noticing their nuances and subtleties. We can also grow in our capacity to develop a vocabulary for these feelings and our ability to gain some objectivity about them. Self-awareness also allows us to observe the thoughts we have about these emotions, engaging our thinking brain along with our emotional brain. It involves going to that place in our brain that gives us the ability to be objective about both thoughts and feelings. We should marvel at the way our brain is able to do this.

The emotionally intelligent pastor functions as though she has a third eye watching her interactions. She is fully aware of her own feelings and also picks up on the feelings of the other person. She may be aware that what this person is saying is making her angry, but she also possesses the EQ skill of self-control. She is able to ask herself if the other person can handle her anger, and if she believes the person cannot, she quiets down and makes sure she does not communicate her anger nonverbally. Her self-awareness also extends to the context of the interaction (perhaps in a meeting with others) and awareness of group process. While attending to both her own and others' thoughts, feelings, and behaviors, she is able to simultaneously participate in the meeting itself and to make wise, emotionally intelligent decisions.

Empathy plays an important role in these interactions. This skill gives this person insight into how other people are feeling about what is transpiring in a group. She might, for example, pick up that two others in the room perceive that she is being unjustly criticized and that the person chairing the meeting holds the opposite perspective. Organizational awareness—understanding how what is taking place in a group affects other people in this congregation—has roots in the skill of empathy.

In addition to self-awareness and empathy, the capacity to manage conflict well also shows up as a strength of effective pastors. When emotions are running high, this pastor has the capacity to ensure that everyone in the meeting is feeling heard, plus she has the ability to lead the group to the best possible resolution of the conflict. The emotionally intelligent pastor realizes that without healthy conflict, creativity is not possible. She helps congregations embrace a process whereby members fight passionately for their perspective to be heard and understood, and then move to some sort of resolution. We talk more about managing conflict in the chapter on stress resilience.

The emotionally intelligent pastor does not need to be skilled in all the emotional intelligence traits as defined by EQ specialists but does need to be proficient enough in many of them to remain an effective spiritual leader. This pastor has the capacity for assertiveness but knows when to be assertive and when to acquiesce. He can tolerate stress and manages his emotions well under pressure. He possesses the EQ trait of independence yet also has the capacity to be adaptable and flexible when the circumstances require that. Beneath all of this is an optimistic perspective on life in general and congregational life in particular.

The perceptions that emotionally intelligent clergy have about themselves are fairly congruent with the views others have of them. This type of accurate self-assessment comes from their capacity to receive feedback from those around them. They actually seek out this feedback, both formally and informally, so they are grounded in how others view them. They are humble, yet self-confident. They have observed how those with unrealistically elevated opinions of themselves are viewed in negative ways by others, but they are also aware that having unnecessarily low opinions of themselves does not serve them well, either. Emotional intelligence is required to manage this balance.

The Capacity to Develop Resonance with Congregants

The ability to develop resonance with other people also grows out of skills in empathy. This capacity allows clergy to sense where other people are emotionally, spiritually, and politically.

Effective pastors have the ability to develop resonance with all congregational members. That is, they can get on the same wavelength with every member of the congregation, as unique as each member is. Clergy who struggle in their relationship with congregational members can usually gain resonance with some members of the congregation but may have strained relationships with others, leaving these others feeling disenfranchised and unappreciated. Such clergy may be clueless as to why they are out of sync with congregational members or fail to see the value of first establishing a solid working relationship with congregants before beginning work with them. In addition, some clergy are simply turned off by certain congregational members and try to avoid them as much as possible. They do not do the hard work of getting beyond their negative impressions of them and work on making a significant emotional connections with them. If we can gain resonance only with congregants we personally like, our effectiveness within congregational life will be limited. Over time, when members have difficulty resonating with their pastor, they leave the congregation, either physically or emotionally. Some stubbornly remain as members but contribute little, whether financially or in terms of participation.

The EQ pastor may have significant political, social, theological, or personality differences with certain members, but he finds some way to connect with all members at an emotional level. Whenever they meet, these members and the clergyperson can smile at each other, because they have discovered some kind of common emotional ground with each other. They have connected at a deep level, which sets the stage for a solid pastoral relationship and allows the pastor to take his members through personal crises or congregational conflict later in life, if need be.

The Emotional Tone of a Congregation

Emotional self-management is vital because it is the pastor who sets the emotional tone for the congregation he serves. That is, the emotional states and actions of the pastor affect how members feel about and experience their congregation. How well clergy manage their own moods and emotions affects everyone else's moods and emotions. Moods and emotions are similar, except that a mood generally lasts for an extended period of time, whereas an emotion is short lived and focuses on a particular situation or experience. Just as the CEO of a corporation sets the emotional tone of the whole company, the pastor sets the emotional tone of the whole congregation, especially the emotional tone of those who work with him on a regular basis. In this way, the emotional intelligence of the pastor greatly influences the kind of emotional intelligence practiced by others within the congregation. This in turn influences how attractive the congregation is to outsiders.

At her core, the EQ pastor is a team player. She may bring fresh, exciting ideas to the congregation, but these ideas are always modified by a team within the congregation so that they can be owned as being "our idea." Timing is everything, and this pastor remains in touch with the emotional tone of the congregation as it relates to a certain issue and thus knows when to press for a decision. Executing brilliant ideas without significant input from the congregation is, in the long run, self-defeating. Because of this, congregational decision making may take much longer, but the execution of such ideas will meet far less resistance from the congregation down the line.

Even if everything else seems just right, when pastors fail to drive the emotions in all dimensions of congregation life in a positive, upbeat direction, some aspect of ministry within the congregation will be truncated. If negative energy is being emitted from, for example, the altar guild, the EQ pastor will find a way to get it back into the positive column. Tension within this small task group can poison other healthy dimensions of congregational life. The EQ pastor either enters the fray to manage this conflict himself or gives oversight to other members who address this conflict.

By offering oversight of the whole congregation, the EQ pastor finds ways to turn negative personal interactions in any dimension of congregational life into healthy, positive ones. Skills in empathy and conflict management assist a pastor in this task.

The Ability to Develop Trust

Trust is central to healthy interactions within a congregation. It begins when a pastor has the capacity to develop trust with all congregational members. When trust exists between pastor and people, the pastor has the potential to develop trust among members. This basic trust allows members to relax when this pastor leads them in worship. When trust is lacking, members find it difficult to enter into the spirit of worship. This basic trust allows the pastor, as preacher, to verbalize some things the congregants may have difficulty hearing. They may disagree with the pastor's perspective, but they will give it serious consideration. A trusted pastor can also influence the kind of openness that exists within task groups when important decisions need to be made.

Yet developing trust can be complicated. Clergy need to be aware that their credibility and behavior are central to pastoral effectiveness. Credibility flows from having both character and competence. Our character is who we are; our competence is what we can do. If we are strong in one area and weak in the other, we won't sustain trust in the long run. A pastor may be beloved by a congregation, but when he consistently demonstrates lack of competence in preaching or leading in worship, members have a hard time trusting him. On the other hand, a pastor may have great skills in preaching and leading others in worship, but when he consistently violates the personal boundaries of congregants, he will also not be trusted.

The Deeper Reason for Developing Significant Relationships

It may appear that we view deeper interpersonal relationships as an end in itself—like developing a warm, friendly country club. Not true! The end product needs to remain the spiritual transformation of members. This means remaining focused on the primary mission of the congregation while deepening the spiritual and emotional connection members feel for one another. Transformed people naturally seek justice, mercy, and peace in the world. They live by forgiveness and are able to forgive others. They continually work at loving their enemies.

We need to remember, however, that transformation is always preceded by nurture. People need to know they are embraced by a caring congregation and pastor when they are challenged to grow spiritually. In the absence of a nurturing environment, the call to change our way of living feels hostile and accusatory. It feels like condemnation rather than an invitation to a more grounded and satisfying life.

Likewise, emotionally intelligent pastors have the capacity to be honest about painful truths that must be addressed if a congregation is to thrive. Because they have established emotional trust, they are able to lead congregations to face controversial issues and to embrace the changes they will need to make to remain relevant to the times and to their immediate community. When a congregational group erupts into toxic emotions, emotionally intelligent pastors have the capacity to intuit where certain negative emotions will resonate in other parts of the system, and they are able to gently lead the group to return to positive interactions with one another. In this way, the pastor acts as the group's emotional guide.

When pastors have gained the respect and trust of their members, people look to them for direction when their congregation is dealing with tough emotional issues. In any kind of congregational crisis, congregants first turn to their pastor to see how she is reacting. Emotionally intelligent clergy are able to remain calm and model a composed approach to the situation. They serve as the emotional anchor in troubled times. In his book *Generation to Generation*, Edwin Friedman talks about the need for a pastor to be a nonanxious presence.[2] In the midst of an anxious congregation, the pastor is able to self-differentiate, and yet remain in contact with these members. As such, pastors have the capacity to help people make sense of a given situation, as troubling as it may be.

The basic task, then, of clergy is to sway everyone's emotions in a positive direction. When a congregation is moved to a state of enthusiasm, significant things begin to happen. The mission and ministry of a congregation will soar. If, on the other hand, a congregation gets bogged down with anxiety and toxic interactions among members, or between the pastor and people, mission and ministry are stifled. When a pastor accepts a call to a congregation that is wallowing in misery, with members interacting in stilted and demeaning ways, her primary task at the beginning is to teach congregation members to support and care for one another, assisting the congregation to become optimistic and enthusiastic about its future. This is a challenging task indeed, and clergy need to understand the emotional cauldron they are entering and know whether they have the EQ capacity to turn it around. Clergy lacking emotional intelligence should refrain from attempting it.

In short, how do we as clergy embody grace in the way we relate to congregants? This is far more complex than simply being "nice" to everyone. There is a certain kind of "niceness" that is not perceived as authentic by congregants. Members pick up on the feeling that their pastor is not being truthful about the way he really feels about them. They may have picked this up from certain nonverbal signs that we have given, or their intuition simply knows that their pastor is not being authentic in his relationships with them. The pastor may be aware of an emotion that has him not liking a certain congregant, and he may try to override that emotion by merely being nice to this person and not engaging in a deeper way. Members see this as a barrier that exists between them and their pastor. In what ways can this pastor be honest about his feelings about a person while still not alienating that person? Authenticity involves our being straight about what is transpiring within us while still remaining connected to another person. We may not be able to be completely honest about our deeper feelings about another person, but authenticity means getting as close as we possibly can while intuiting how much of our honesty the person can take. It is an art and can be seen as a dance we have with each individual congregant. In the long run, this way of relating to congregants embodies the grace that we preach to them verbally. We need to struggle to be the grace we proclaim. This requires great emotional intelligence on our part.

How to Become an Emotionally Intelligent Pastor

Given the importance of emotional intelligence for the pastor, we have to ask: How do we acquire emotional intelligence in the first place? The starting place, of course, is our family of origin. Some people are lucky enough to be born into a family system that is a healthy, emotionally stable system. This does not mean that there aren't blowups or scenes that are pretty ugly emotionally. Over the long haul, however, a reasonably healthy family system deals with these crises, and members of the family continue to have affection for each other.

We have to acknowledge that families fall on a continuum between emotionally healthy and nurturing and self-destructive and abusive. We need to work with the family we were given. Whatever cards we were dealt, our success in life depends on what we do with what we have learned in our family of origin and how we can build on that. People who did not experience positive relationships in their family of origin will need to find other communities that can teach them how to live emotionally intelligent lives. Much depends upon our capacity to search out new relationships with people who have the potential to teach us the positive interpersonal skills that are required for success in most careers and in our personal lives.

Those called to the ordained ministry include individuals from across the spectrum of families of origin. There are no data that indicate that men and women from abusive, exploitive families of origin are unable to carry out effective ministry in congregations. Some people have the capacity to become wounded healers, utilizing their negative experiences in their family of origin to become beloved pastors of congregations. Their journey toward emotional health may have involved some painful and challenging learning experiences, but they have moved steadily toward a more balanced and mature emotional state. Some people who have come from dysfunctional families of origin may find a congregation that exhibits positive emotional traits, and they acquire some emotionally intelligent skills in that setting. Pastors and leaders within congregations need to view this as yet another reason to become an emotionally intelligent congregation.

Others enter into personal friendships with people who assist them in developing positive interpersonal skills. Still others find places of employment that exhibit a positive EQ environment and have learned EQ in that setting. Some may have lucked out by belonging to a school system that taught them how to develop positive relations with others. Others may have had schoolteachers who took them under their wings and coached them on how to develop a cadre of friends. For the most part, however, the whole spectrum of interpersonal relationships will be much more of a challenge for people not having grown up in positive home environments.

Whatever our experience growing into adulthood, we are all challenged to progress in our journey to becoming even more emotionally intelligent church professionals. As we stated at the beginning of this chapter, "it is all about relationships." Wherever we are on the EQ continuum, what are some concrete things we can do for ourselves to move us more deeply into emotional health? Here are some suggestions.

Clinical Pastoral Education (CPE)

Of all the requirements seminaries and denominations have for would-be clergy, this one has the greatest potential for increasing emotional intelligence. Students are challenged to get out of their heads and face the emotions that surface as they try to embody grace and care while relating to people in a hospital or other ministry setting that deals with a whole spectrum of physical and emotional ailments. Dealing with these feelings with other CPE students and a CPE supervisor can be a real emotional awakening for many. CPE students can come from all types of denominational seminaries, and, regardless of their theology or biblical orientation, they are challenged to become more aware of their emotions and how these emotions affect their relationships with patients and fellow students. CPE has been a life-changing experience for many students. Taking a quarter of CPE is a good beginning, but staying on for another three or nine months would be even better.

Psychotherapy

During times of emotional turmoil or trauma, working with a therapist can begin a healing process. Yet we do not need to wait until we encounter emotional difficulty to engage a therapist. In many ways, we can be almost as much of a mystery to ourselves as God is a mystery to us. Entering into this mystery with the help of a professional therapist can be a great gift. In the safety of a trusted professional relationship, we can explore emotions we have suppressed for years. A therapist can also assist us to come to terms with difficult family relationships that have troubled us for a long time.

Entering into a therapeutic process has the potential to increase our self-awareness and leading us to realistic but positive self-regard. The emotional traits of emotional expression and emotional self-control can also be enhanced. Should we be depressed, therapy can move us to develop a more positive outlook on life. It can increase our capacity for relationship management and conflict management. Should our assertiveness or lack of it be an issue, this can also be addressed, along with our impulse control.

Pastor/Parish Relations Committees

By its very title, this committee makes great emotional intelligence sense. This is a small group of people who take on the task of maintaining a healthy relationship between the pastor and the congregation. Why is that important? The ordained ministry can be a lonely role for those in it, and many feel isolated in it because they perceive that no one in the congregation really understands what they go through on a day-to-day basis. Every congregation will probably have a small group of people who can grasp the complexity of this role and a few who are willing to work at trying to understand it. There are certain dimensions that need to be managed well if such a committee is to work. Congregations that manage it well are in the minority. There are six conditions under which such a committee can be useful to a pastor.

a) These committees need to be structured such that the pastor can trust the intentions of the people in that group. Without trust, that pastor will be unwilling to share the pain and vulnerability of her role. The confidentiality of what is shared needs also to be understood. If what is shared on this committee becomes the subject of the gossip in the congregation, that will be the last time the pastor shares anything of substance with the group. In several denominations, people are elected to that role with the pastor having very little input as to who should get elected. What would motivate people to allow themselves to be elected to such a committee? Some may truly like the pastor and want to be as supportive as possible, while others are unhappy with the way the pastor is executing her role and want the power to get her to function better. We cannot expect a pastor to trust the work of such a committee if some in that group are there to try to "fix" her.

b) We know of one denomination that allows the pastor to choose two of the four people on that committee, with the governing board choosing the other two. If one of the two persons assigned by the board to this committee sees his role as that of making sure the congregation gets its money's worth out of this pastor, that pastor's trust of this committee will be low. We would opt for the pastor choosing six to eight people he feels he could work with on that committee with the board choosing four from the ones suggested. The trust level between pastor and committee has a better chance under such an arrangement.

c) Up front, such a committee will need to expend time and energy in first understanding what it is like being a pastor in the congregation. The best way to do this is to have the pastor log every thirty minutes of his workday over the course of two weeks. The items logged in this way can be placed into categories. It is usually a surprise to a committee when they study such an accounting. Most are amazed that their pastor puts in a whole lot more hours per week than they expected. The committee will also learn how certain members consume inordinate amounts of the pastor's time, plus all the hours he has to put into keeping peace in the congregation. Once this committee has learned what it is really like being the pastor of this congregation, they have the potential to be a major source of support and perspective for their pastor.

d) The committee needs to develop a way to listen to and manage the complaints and criticism members have of their pastor. Some of these complaints need to be shared with the pastor while others should not even be mentioned. Some complaints come from malcontents who will never be placated. Other complaints are off base, while still others are totally unrealistic. The committee needs to decide what are some realistic expectations of their pastor in relation to these complaints.

e) The committee needs to be consultative in nature without having decision-making powers. They should be accountable to the governing board and make periodic recommendations to that board about ways the congregation can best utilize the gifts and graces of this pastor. They can also make recommendations about ways in which the congregation can best support the pastor's health and wholeness, plus her having quality time with family (if married).

f) And the committee needs to resist tasks laid upon it by the governing board that run counter to the basic purpose of supporting the pastor, such as conducting the annual review of the pastor. A pastor will be reluctant to share pain and vulnerability if she knows this same group of people will oversee her annual evaluation, especially if such an annual review will determine her salary. The committee also needs to resist being the congregation's personnel committee.

Structuring a P/PR committee in these ways gives it a better chance of really being a supportive and useful group to the pastor. Trust levels may rise and fall over the years. When such a committee becomes untrustworthy to the pastor, it will just be another committee meeting for her to attend—its usefulness is lost. Someone on the governing board needs to have a clear vision of the usefulness of such a committee and the way it needs to be set up to work well.

Someone looking at the way we recommend setting up a pastor/parish relations committee may say, "When the pastor is able to appoint only her friends to the committee, they will never share anything negative with her about her ministry." We don't believe that. A pastor's friends will want her to succeed. If she is doing something that is stupid and alienates congregants, the committee is going to tell her about it. Because they want to help her be effective, they will let her know how members are interpreting her behavior and why such behavior is self-defeating. Accurate self-assessment occurs when the opinion the pastor has about herself is fairly congruent with how others perceive her. This can rarely happen without the pastor receiving feedback from congregants and colleagues. In terms of emotional intelligence, the pastor needs to have a healthy self-regard in order to ask for and be open to the feedback of others. The pastor/parish relations committee can be one specific channel for making the feedback of congregants relevant to the way the pastor is executing his or her role in the congregation.

Clergy Support Groups

As noted above, because the role of parish pastor is so complex, laypeople often have little understanding of that role. For this reason, clergy need support from professional colleagues. Establishing relationships with fellow clergy is not easy, because casual contacts with colleagues in ministry can degenerate into complaining and bragging ("the bitch and brag syndrome"). Complaining and bragging are so easy to do because they require little risk. What we need, however, is to be with colleagues with whom we can share our pain and vulnerability. We need to be able to explore with other clergy experiences that frighten or confuse us. This requires a context in which the trust level is high. We don't usually share pain and confusion with people we relate to in a casual way, as clergy often do at judicatory-related functions.

Emotionally healthy clergy put effort into forming clergy groups that have a high level of trust among its members. To begin such a group, clergy should identify one other clergyperson (regardless of denomination) with whom they would feel free to share their pain and vulnerability. They then need to meet with that person to explore the possibility of forming a supportive clergy group. Should they agree on which other clergy they both could trust with their vulnerability, these other church professionals need to be invited into the peer support group. A support group of four to six people is quite enough and ensures everyone will have significant airtime.

The next step is very important. We recommend hiring a facilitator to convene the group for a period of time, at least the first six months. This person should receive some remuneration, so he and the group remain clear about his role. Research that Roy has done on clergy support systems indicates that the chances of developing a group that demonstrates trust quadruples when the group is led by a trusted facilitator.[3] Without an outside facilitator, someone in the group will need to assume a leadership role, diminishing the support he or she might receive from the group. If a group tries to rotate the leadership role, the group will flounder, because everyone's leadership style is different. In particular, if someone has a laid-back leadership style, members of the group may experience themselves as being leaderless. Possible group facilitators may include chaplains, CPE supervisors, social service personnel, or retired clergy. We do recommend, however, that the facilitator will have spent some time as a parish pastor. Without that experience, the person may have simplistic notions of that special role. Once such a group develops the kind of trust that is needed for deep personal sharing, the need for such an outside facilitator may diminish. If, however, one of its members moves and the group decides to invite others into the group, the whole dynamic of the group changes, and they may once again need to hire an outside facilitator who brings safety, structure, and order to the group.

Emotional Intelligence Workshops

One of the chief reasons Roy and colleagues formed the Center for EQ-HR Skills is to combine the latest developments in emotional intelligence with human relations training. This training is priced to make it affordable to church professionals and is available in workshops around the country. More information is available at www.eqhrcenter.org.

Spiritual Disciplines

Effective pastors build into their daily lives times and places where they can check in on what emotions are dominating their lives. These are disciplines and rituals that continually engage them in greater self-awareness. This is where the practice of meditation or keeping a journal can assist in this task.

Meditation, in its many forms, is taught all over the world, within many spiritual traditions, and they all contribute to the emotionally intelligent trait of self-awareness. In North America, many people use meditation as a stress-management tool, and most books on holistic health claim this is one of the healthiest things we can do for ourselves. Within certain religious traditions, the practice of meditation is called contemplative prayer. The basis of contemplative prayer is learning how to listen to God—to be open to experiencing the presence of God in the here and now. We learn to listen to God by first listening to ourselves—staying present to thoughts, feelings, and physical sensations and not getting hooked by them. We then learn to discern whether there is a subtle message from God in what we are hearing.

Reflective writing, which is more than just keeping a diary of the events of our day, has the potential to upgrade our EQ as well. It is another way of increasing self-awareness about what we are feeling in the moment as well as throughout different events in our day. *At a Journal Workshop*[4] by Ira Progoff is a helpful book in this regard.

Coaches

Working with a coach or EQ specialist to assist us in dealing with emotionally laden situations on the job or in our life can lead to much better management of these occasions.[5]

Personality Surveys

A number of personality surveys have the potential to increase self-awareness and self-understanding, which will raise our EQ. These are most effective if we work through the results with someone trained to administer them. The Myers-Briggs Type Indicator is the most popular worldwide, with research to document its accuracy and effectiveness. The Enneagram has also been a useful personality assessment instrument to others. Its surveys are not nearly as accurate as the MBTI, but its value in self-understanding is high. There are close to a dozen helpful books on the Enneagram, and it takes time and motivation to wade through one or two before being able to identify oneself within nine possible types. It has been the experience of many who have identified their Enneagram number that they have been led into significant self-insight. It is their default way of thinking and perceiving that shapes how they approach relationships and life.

Diversity or Multicultural Training

All of us at some point in our lives need to confront our various prejudices. We all have different ones, depending on how we were acculturated.

In-depth exposure to ethnic, racial, gender, or sexual diversity would have the potential to confront our prejudices and lead us to greater emotional intelligence. An academic approach to such prejudices has minimal effect unless the plight of these people can be dramatically made clear. We need to change people's hearts as well as their minds.

Anger Management Workshops

If we can recall relationships that were destroyed because of our anger or work settings in which our anger with a coworker diminished our effectiveness, we may benefit from a course on anger management—preferably in a face-to-face setting rather than online.

Becoming an emotionally intelligent pastor is a lifelong process. All of us have some EQ, as we never start at zero. Yet just because we grow older does not automatically ensure that we are increasing our EQ. This requires hard, intentional work. It will test our capacity to reflect on all our intrapersonal, interpersonal, intergroup exchanges and review how we might handle them more wisely. In addition, however, we need to be motivated to get better at this. The old saying that "we learn by experience" is not true. We learn only from experience that we reflect on in a disciplined way.

The payoff for increasing our EQ can be tremendous. Whatever we do to increase our EQ will result in our having a more successful career and a more satisfying personal life. Bottom line, it is all about relationships. What can be more satisfying than quality relationships all around?

TWELVE

Implications for Transition Points in Ministry

There are transition points in ministry where there are more intense interactions between people, making emotional intelligence especially crucial. These are mainly transition points in the various stages of clergy/congregational relationships, and there are some that are unique to clergy and some unique to congregations alone. There are two words that capture well transitions within human life—these are "danger" and "opportunity." These transition points are moments pregnant with possibility, but they are also times when things can go terribly wrong. New beginnings often require great amounts of energy and enthusiasm, but they are also times when human interactions can get off to a bad start. As the saying goes, "We don't get a second chance to make a first impression." When the deep relationships that should develop at these juncture points in ministry don't develop, opportunities are lost, and congregational life experiences a setback.

Transition Points for Clergy

1. Starting up in a new congregation
2. Terminating a pastoral relationship with a congregation

137

3. Recruiting laypersons to consider the ordained ministry: selecting persons with strong emotional intelligence
4. Transition from seminary culture into one's first congregation

Transition Points within Congregational Life

1. Closing out ministry with one pastor, experiencing an interim period, and welcoming in a new pastor
2. Congregations moving from one size to another
3. Assimilating new members: the transition into membership

Starting Up in a New Congregation

Some forty years ago, the Alban Institute was launched after Loren Mead completed a study within the Episcopal Church called Project Test Pattern. The material that grew out of that study was called *Prime Time for Renewal*, as they discovered great opportunities for congregational revitalization when a congregation called a new priest. Later, Alban specialized in assisting clergy and congregations traverse other transitions in ministry with publications written on all the transition points listed above.

Underneath all the research and program development at the Alban Institute was the basic assumption that clergy and congregational members possessed skills in relationship development. It was a shaky assumption. Alban program proposals worked well for laypeople and church professionals who possessed some basic skills in emotional intelligence. For those who lacked these fundamental skills, however, there was usually trouble brewing. Either clergy were lacking in their capacity for emotionally intelligent interactions with congregational members or they simply did not perceive the development of these relationships as important.

UCC pastor and church consultant Howard Friend wrote an article for Alban's magazine, *Congregations*, titled "Failure to Form Basic Partnership: Resolving a Dilemma of New Pastorates."[1] The basic point in this article has to do with his experience of being asked to consult in congregations that were in conflict with their pastors. As he probed deeper into the background of this conflict, he often discovered that the pastor and the congregation had not formed a positive partnership years back when the pastor first arrived. Now, some three to five years later, that early lack of partnership was finally resulting in problems. It is difficult to try to restore a relationship between pastor and people that never existed in the first place. Friend concludes that a basic sense of trust between pastor and people had not existed right from the beginning. It takes large amounts of emotional intelligence to develop a relationship of trust with a congregation, and these clergy either didn't have the skill and integrity to pull it off or did not see it as important in their pastoral ministry.

The EQ Needed When Pastors Start Up in a New Congregation

When congregants meet their new pastor, of utmost importance to them is the question "Is this pastor going to like me?" Many times, this is an unconscious question, but it is that basic. A mistake we clergy often make is thinking the congregation wants mainly to view our competence, so we focus on trying to impress them with our skills and abilities rather than on being genuinely interested in them as persons. What will impress them instead is our intent to get to know each of them more deeply.

In "Clergy Start Up" workshops for the Alban Institute, which Roy ran, he would often have attendees, on an afternoon off, go to a shopping center and just sit and watch people. They were to decide, as they locked in on an individual, whether they liked that person or not. They were to go further and become clear as to why they either liked him or disliked him. This was a tune-up for their becoming clearer about their personal preferences in other people.

We clergy are human like everyone else—we like certain people and don't like others. No doubt, we will meet people in our new congregation whom we will not naturally like. Without awareness of our reactions to people, we might inadvertently convey nonverbal expressions that say to them, "I really don't like you." Can we imagine what this would be like for a congregant who gets the sense that "my new pastor really doesn't like me"? "For the next ten years, possibly longer, I'm going to be in a congregation where the pastor doesn't like me." Once again, it is all about relationships.

Connecting Deeply with One's Predecessor

Often clergy moving to another congregation avoid extended contact with their predecessor. We are one of the few professions that try to remain disinterested in our predecessor's experience with people. It is as though we do not want to be prejudiced by the former pastor's relationships with congregants. Clergy often say, "I want to be free to form my own impressions of people." There may be some merit in that stance, but we can make the mistake of allowing ourselves to be blindsided by the reactions of some congregants to us. We would be much better prepared if we knew:

- the names of people who were the most troublesome to the former pastor;
- the names of people she could usually count on for support on important decisions and to whom she could turn when personally discouraged;
- who were the "power" people in the congregation—namely, the people to whom other congregants looked when an important decision was needed;
- who were the people who were part of the leadership core but drifted to the periphery during her ministry;
- what were her primary reasons for leaving the congregation; and
- who are the people that will miss her the most.

If relationships are central to an effective ministry, why would we not want to get as much information about people as we can as we enter a new congregation?

Connecting More Deeply with the Search/Call Committee

Those who have served on a search/call committee know what a demanding role that can be. Some committees, especially from larger congregations, when they begin their assigned tasks, go on a weekend retreat just to do some team building, to determine everyone's assumptions about the kind of pastor the congregation needs now. Denominations usually require such a committee to do a congregational self-study before giving them names of clergy who might be a match for them. This is followed by wading through a wide variety of candidate résumés to find someone who might suit their congregation. These committees have been known to meet weekly for a year or more before making their final recommendation to the governing board. They will be exhausted, but they will also miss connecting in meaningful ways with other people on that committee in the future. They will have experienced the five stages of community development described by Scott Peck. The incoming pastor would do well to meet with them early on in the new pastorate. She would be wise to find a way to celebrate the work of the committee and explore ways they might stay in touch. The committee might act as the pastor's confidant regarding how people are responding to her ministry. Without such communication, it is not uncommon for people on the search/call committee to leave the congregation within two years of the new pastor arriving. Some of this may be because the new pastor is not working out as they expected, and they are feeling guilty about the decision they made to call this pastor. They may feel that other congregants blame them for making a poor choice in a new pastor. Another reason could be that they were somebody of importance in the congregation when serving on the "search committee," but when the new pastor arrived, they became a "nobody." Much of their intense work was invisible to other congregational members. Mostly, they just missed the close, intense working relationship they had with other members on the committee. An emotionally intelligent congregation would do well to monitor the life of these committee members in the months following the closure of this group.

The Psychological Contract Members Seek with Their New Pastor

When becoming better acquainted with congregants, a new but emotionally intelligent pastor can begin searching for the psychological contract members would like with her. This contract is somewhat akin to marriage—both parties have expectations of the other, and both are committed to giving the other person what is expected.

There really are two psychological contracts involved here—one that the member has with the congregation and another with the pastor. These contracts, which are largely unconscious, will begin to show up in initial conversations and will possibly become clearer with time. Members, after all, are entering into some type of contract with a new spiritual leader. Much may be expected by some members and very little by others. Some examples may help: One member may communicate in overt or subtle ways that he is and will be very active in congregational life and expects a strong supportive relationship with the pastor. In so many words, this member may be saying, "I'm going to be serving on various committees in the church, I'll likely be attending church services three Sundays out of four, and I expect a lot of your personal time and attention." Another congregant may be saying, in so many words, "Pastor, you are going to see me only infrequently in church. Don't ask me to serve on any task group.

I don't expect you to be calling on me. Please bury me when I die." The difference between these two members is huge. The emotionally intelligent pastor needs to treat each of these congregants in radically different ways. This is why having some idea of this psychological contract is important. When people are unhappy with the pastor and the church, it is because this contract has been broken in some way. They expected something to happen and it didn't, or something happened that should not have. When these contracts are broken, from the perspective of the congregant, the person may feel he has the right to renegotiate his relationship with the congregation. He may decide he will no longer attend to congregational obligations such as showing up at services or contributing money.

A pastor new to a congregation, knowing that these psychological contracts exist with every member, will be looking for the symbolic gestures or stories that give the pastor some clues about that preferred contract. Whenever a congregant tells about an incident that took place between him and a former pastor, he is saying either "I'd like you to be like this" or "I hope you are not that kind of pastor." In the beginning, when the new pastor spends some one-on-one time with a congregant, she should be able to return to her car and write out, on a three-by-five card, her sense of the psychological contract that person wants with her and an ongoing one with the congregation. When trying to get to know a congregant and to unearth this contract, the pastor might begin to ask a different set of questions. Much of the contract could be hidden in other relationships the person has had with former pastors, so it is a good idea to ask a congregant to reflect openly with the new pastor on these former pastoral relationships. Clues to a congregant's psychological contracts may be contained in these past relationships.

With the skill of bringing the psychological contract to the surface also comes the capacity to engage in contract negotiation or renegotiation. For example, the pastor may be visiting one of the congregation's shut-ins and be clued in on the fact that this person expects to be visited by the pastor monthly. Probably, she had that kind of relationship with a former pastor. If the new pastor realizes that this is simply asking too much, a negotiation conversation may have the pastor saying something like "Mabel, I normally visit my shut-ins once a quarter. Is that going to be enough for you to still consider me to be a good pastor?"

Knowing that such a contract exists with every congregant, entering into a type of contract negotiation is emotionally intelligent. It is building a type of relationship that serves most of a congregant's need, yet allows the pastor to sustain those relationships with integrity. A new pastor who makes promises to certain congregants at this level but knows she will not fulfill those promises lacks, and her relationships will suffer.

Pastoral ministry really is all about relationships. It needs to be the major focus of the new pastor in those opening months of a new pastorate. Moving too quickly to make changes in the congregation without first establishing these relationships will get this new pastorate off to a bad start.

Starting Up in Different-Size Congregations

Building relationships within a new congregation needs to involve different people depending upon the size of the congregation. Four sizes are commonly discussed. Each of these four sizes requires a different type of leadership from its pastor, hence the need to focus on different people within each size congregation.

FAMILY-SIZE CONGREGATION
(WORSHIP ATTENDANCE OF FEWER THAN FIFTY EACH SUNDAY)

In small-membership congregations with worship attendance below fifty, the most important relationship will be between the pastor and the matriarch/patriarch of the congregation. Small congregations usually have high pastoral turnover, making for longer and more frequent periods of time when no pastor is present. Lay leaders need to take hold of the leadership needs of the congregation during these times of pastoral vacancy. Congregants will likely come to respect and appreciate their taking on that role. A pastor entering into such a congregation needs to realize how central this role is of the patriarch or matriarch to the congregation. She needs to know that she is not in control of the congregation and that any changes she might like to make in the congregation need first to be approved by the patriarch or matriarch. Should she ignore this basic norm and try to initiate a change in the congregation, all eyes will turn first to the matriarch. If she doesn't like the proposal, other congregants will not support it. Knowing that clergy come and go easily in their size congregation, the matriarch is not likely to let the congregation get stuck with a program that the congregation can't support once the pastor leaves—and they don't expect the pastor to stay for any significant length of time.

Knowing the centrality of the patriarch's or matriarch's role in the congregation, the incoming pastor needs to work especially hard on developing a relationship with this person. This will not be easy, as the two of them may be miles apart as to how the congregation is to be run and what needs to happen to help the congregation thrive. Building a working relationship with the patriarch or matriarch will take all the emotional intelligence a new pastor can muster. It is going to take years before this dynamic will change. It will change when the pastor has been around for a few years, five at the least, and people begin to trust the new pastor as much as the patriarch/matriarch.

Since this size congregation is made up of family units that cluster together to support the congregation, the new pastor needs to be seen as part of these family units—and more than likely there will be some contention between these families that will need to be managed by the pastor. The new pastor needs to be seen as not taking sides in these interfamily connections.

THE PASTORAL-SIZE CONGREGATION (WORSHIP ATTENDANCE BETWEEN 50 AND 150)

This size congregation can afford a decent salary for its clergyperson, and clergy usually stay for much longer periods of time. There is great potential for the relationship between pastor and people to develop into something strong and lasting. The congregation is also of a size that the pastor is able to develop a deep relationship with everyone in the congregation, visiting some people in their homes. The pastor may have some great ideas about how this congregation can grow and expand on its ministry, but changes should not be introduced until there is a solid relationship between pastor and people. In short, avoid changes within the congregation for the first nine to twelve months, but the first change needs to be something of substance that will move this congregation forward and not something that is merely cosmetic or simply a favorite program of the pastor. It is going to take time to really understand what changes need to come first. It is important for the new pastor to make those changes only after having developed a solid relationship with all members.

In this size congregation, the spiritual needs of members are usually met by a personal relationship with the pastor. Little spiritual growth will take place when the relationship between a congregant and the pastor is not one of trust. With some people, building that kind of trust will take time and consistent effort. Often pastors will find that building these relationships brings them joy and career satisfaction. This kind of pastoral role is possibly what called them into the ordained ministry in the first place, and clergy should consider staying in pastoral-size congregations for their entire career if a personal relationship with congregants is what gives them greatest satisfaction.[2] Clergy who work well within pastoral-size congregations generally do not do well when called to program- or corporate-size congregations. They will attempt to function in a program-size congregation as in a pastoral-size one, only on a larger scale. When this happens, the congregation is not likely to grow spiritually or numerically. There are simply too many members in larger congregations to take care of in this way. Pastors hooked on pastoral-size ministries, when moved to larger congregations, may unconsciously simply wait until the congregation shrinks in size so they can manage it well at a reduced size.

THE PROGRAM-SIZE CONGREGATION
(WORSHIP ATTENDANCE BETWEEN 150 AND 350)

When worship attendance reaches 150 or more every Sunday, total membership is probably between three hundred and five hundred. With this number of congregants to serve, having people's spiritual needs met through a personal relationship with the pastor is unrealistic. Instead, the spiritual needs of members are met through programs. The primary inter-personal connections that need to be made between pastor and members are with those laypeople who are in leadership roles within the congrega-tion offering leadership to these programs. Relationships with these peo-ple, and the leadership they give to congregational programs, need to be a greater priority for the new pastor than the individual pastoral care needs of members.

This by no means implies that the pastoral care of members becomes unimportant. It remains of great importance, but this ministry needs to come from both the pastor and a cadre of laypeople with skills in listening and praying with others. In other words, this size congregation needs to foster a pastoral care team that is supported by the pastor but not man-aged by him alone. This will entail discovering congregants whose emo-tional intelligence is strong and coaching them to use these EQ skills when ministering to other members experiencing a personal crisis.

To begin with, the new pastor will need to personally visit all home-bound people first to develop a relationship with them; members of the pastoral care team will handle most future visits. Periodically, shut-ins will receive a phone call from the pastor inquiring how lay visitors are caring for them. This is going to be a challenge for clergy who love doing pastoral care and are good at it. Can their skill and enthusiasm for pastoral care be translated into training other lay leaders to do much of it?

THE CORPORATE-SIZE CONGREGATION
(WORSHIP ATTENDANCE OF 350 AND HIGHER)

When moving into this size congregation, the emotionally intelligent pastor will focus first on building a solid relationship with staff members and second with the "power" people in the congregation. The challenge for the new pastor will be to build a team that will work as a unit in meeting the administrative and the program needs of the congregation. This will require much time spent on team building with staff members. The called pastor needs to learn how to offer quality ministry to congregants through other people. Staff members who are not willing to be part of the team with the new pastor may need to resign. The rule needs to be "Either become a team player or go." If and when new or replacement staff members are hired, in addition to bringing varieties of skills and abilities to the congregation, these new staff members need to be selected for their skills in working as part of a team with other staff members. All staff members will need to have some skills in emotional intelligence, including bookkeepers and business managers, but those with program responsibilities will need large amounts of it. In addition to their ministry specialty, they should be hired for their EQ depth.

Next, a new pastor in a corporate-size congregation needs to develop a trusting relationship with all the power people in the congregation. A discreet conversation with several lay leaders whom the new pastor trusts will surface the identity of the congregation's most respected and influential people. Without a supportive relationship with these people, a new pastor will be spinning his wheels in the sand. These are the people who need to be on the pastor's side when controversy strikes—and usually something controversial needs to take place if the congregation's ministry is to deepen and expand. Building relationships with these two groups of people will occupy the new pastor's first nine to twelve months before major changes are to be initiated.

Terminating a Pastoral Relationship with a Congregation

As challenging as it is to first establish deep relationships within a congregation, closing out those relationships can be just as complex. When moving to another congregation or moving into retirement, a pastor who just walks out of people's lives without a meaningful closure with them is going to leave some of them deeply wounded. We cannot expect that laypeople will ever again enter into a deep relationship with a future pastor if they have their heart continually broken by the way former clergy terminated their relationship with them.

In research completed by Roy on the way army chaplains left a congregation to be assigned to another one, he found that five out of seven chaplains diminished their ministry by the way they left their congregations. Laypeople were saying to themselves, "We thought our chaplain cared about us, but by the way he left I'm not sure anymore." A nickname the army has for such a chaplain is "bridge cutter." Once this chaplain had been assigned to a different post, he did not seek out ways to close out significant relationships that had developed and for the most part became unavailable to members.

The relationship a pastor develops with every congregant will be unique to that individual. Superior emotional intelligence is required to know how to have a meaningful closure with each of these members. Depending upon the size of the congregation, this means that some members (all members in a family- or pastoral-size congregation) will need to receive some individual time with the departing pastor. Such a closure time will include some reflection on the part of both pastor and member on the history and nature of their relationship. This needs to include all the ups and downs of that relationship, not just reflection on the up times. What will each person miss or not miss? At the end of such a time of reflection, a brief ritual to celebrate that relationship may be observed. This may simply be a time of prayer, or something special to drink, or just a hug. Every congregant with a deep relationship to the pastor will need to know how they have contributed to the joy of their pastor's ministry. If, however, the relationship between the pastor and a congregant has been a rocky one throughout the pastor's tenure, an effective closure process may have these two people reflecting on what went wrong in their relationship and whether it could have ended on a more positive note. What did each person learn because of that relationship?

In a larger congregation, some congregants will at least receive a special phone call from the departing pastor in addition to some getting a personal visit. Then there are work groups within the congregation that will take some time to reflect on the working relationship they have had with the departing pastor. Other congregants will receive a special handwritten note from the pastor. Before leaving, there can be parts of sermons that convey what the departing pastor is feeling about leaving the congregation. These considerations are all part of a pastor terminating his relationships with congregants in an emotionally intelligent way. We know this occurs when both the departing pastor and the congregants being left end up in an emotionally healthy place.

Pastors moving from this pastorate into retirement, particularly if this last pastorate has been a long one and the relationship has been positive and productive, may choose to announce their resignation three to five years in advance. Along with such an announcement would be the request that these last years be the best ever, involving plans that will be accomplished before the final departure. In the past, Roy has conducted workshops titled "Finishing Strong, Ending Well," focused on a rich and meaningful closure for long-term pastorates. Attendees were clergy who wanted to enter retirement at the top of their game rather than slowly petering out. Usually, congregations valued highly such a contract because they expected that, as their pastor neared retirement age, they would receive a resignation letter and their pastor would be gone in three months. They valued having that amount of advance notice, knowing that they could count on their pastor staying around for an extended period of time. They could also plan on a more meaningful closure process with their pastor. If congregational ministry is all about relationships, the recommended closure processes will manage relationships with care, even as these ministries are closed out.

As a rule of thumb for how much time should be set aside for a closure process, we suggest one week of closure time for every year of the departing pastor's tenure. Yes, the pastor who has been with the congregation for twenty years should consider doing nothing but closure work for the last five months of that ministry.

Recruiting Laypersons to Consider the Ordained Ministry: Selecting Persons with Strong Emotional Intelligence

The May 1, 2013, edition of the *Wall Street Journal* carried an article titled "B-Schools Know How You Think, But How Do You Feel?" The article cites a number of business schools that are now testing applicants in emotional intelligence as well as academic résumés. Subtitled "Forget What You Know. Business Schools Increasingly Want to Know What You Feel," the article continues:

> Measuring EQ—or emotional intelligence quotient—is the latest attempt by business schools to identify future stars. Since students

typically start their job hunts almost as soon as they arrive on campus, these schools have little time to fix any faults. "Companies select for top talent with assessment like this," says Andrew Sama, senior associate director of M.B.A. admissions at University of Notre Dame's Mendoza College of Business. "If we are selecting for future business leaders, why shouldn't we use similar tools?"[3]

If business schools are now testing potential students in EQ skills before admission, how much more important would testing the EQ of potential seminary students be? If congregational life is all about relationships, an effective pastor will need as much emotional intelligence as any corporate CEO. If business schools identify future stars because of a student's high EQ, should not denominational screening committees seek out similar characteristics?

With the strong case we hope we are making about having emotionally intelligent pastors serving congregations if they are to thrive, we have some idea as to how a denomination can screen for such people in their recruitment efforts.

The technology is already in place that can test for such traits. Currently, there are two comprehensive surveys on emotional intelligence that are popular in testing an individual's EQ (the Hay Group's 360 Emotional and Social Competency Inventory and the Multi-Health System's EQ-i 2.0-360). There are many more EQ surveys on the market, but most are not field-tested like these two, and both have revised and updated their surveys within the past twelve months. Either one could provide EQ data that would aid in the selection of ministerial candidates. In the EQ-360 surveys, up to twenty other people assess an individual in addition to that person's own assessment. This test results in a thirty-five-page printout of the person's emotional intelligence skills. The survey report contains graphs comparing how the individual rated himself with how all the other people rated him. For example, the report will compare how individuals rated themselves as opposed to how they were rated by their

- manager
- direct reports
- peers
- clients/congregants
- family members
- others (people who don't fit any of the above categories)

With the exception of their manager, there will be at least three people in each of the remaining categories, preserving the anonymity of their raters. Research indicates that when the results of a survey will influence people being hired or not hired for a job, individuals will often rate themselves higher than is realistic. In an EQ-360 survey, an individual's high scores will show up when compared with how others rate him or her. People with an accurate self-assessment will have scores that are similar to how other people have rated them. Wouldn't we all like our pastor to have accurate self-assessment rather than one with low self-regard or one having an excessively high self-regard?

It is our conviction that it is the emotional intelligence of an individual that will determine her effectiveness or lack of it as an ordained parish pastor. Denominations may want to include other surveys, like the MBTI, MMPI (Minnesota Multiphasic Personality Inventory), and so forth, to determine other concerns they might have about candidates, but the key survey should be the one on emotional intelligence.

When those who feel called to the ordained ministry score low on emotional intelligence, denominations need not disqualify them completely. Emotional intelligence is something that can be acquired. There are places such an individual can go to acquire competence in these traits. It will not be easy, but it is possible. It may take several years, but the door is not completely closed to such an applicant. The great thing about emotional intelligence is that it can be learned over time. When one is intentional about acquiring these skills, that time can be shortened. Quite possibly an individual may not have acquired those skills in his or her family of origin and so will have to learn them over time in other social settings.

When a regional body's screening committee needs to turn down a person's application because of low EQ scores, that committee will have something concrete to say to that person. In his original research on regional body screening committees, resulting in the book published by Alban, *Finding Leaders for Tomorrow's Church*,[4] Roy found that members of such committees knew intuitively that a certain person should not be admitted to the ordination track at that time, but they were often at a loss for something concrete to say to the person being turned down. With the results of an EQ-360 survey available to them, they would have much to talk about as to what was needed before the person would be considered ready for the ordained ministry.

An individual having low scores in an EQ-360 survey has a potential road map as to how to do better on such a survey. He will be able to see graphs that point to deficiencies in twelve or fifteen EQ capacities, depending upon the survey utilized. He can be given some guidance how to upgrade his skills in those areas.

Getting into therapy would assist him in this quest, as would attending one or several workshops on emotional intelligence and human relations skills. Acquiring the discipline of daily or frequent journaling would help, as would be having a spiritual director. Taking a course in anger management would help, if anger or impulse control is an issue. Receiving training in the skill of meditation or contemplative prayer and observing the discipline daily would also help, as would being part of an intentional support group. Where possible, hiring a coach could do much to increase one's emotional intelligence.

Screening committees for ordained ministry have a grave responsibility, and we, the authors, are for giving them all the tools they need. The decision to turn down an aspirant may devastate that person, and committee members may feel the personal pain of that person, but ultimately this will be saving such a person much heartache if it is clear that he or she will struggle in the ordained role. Without adequate emotional intelligence, these people will not have a satisfying experience as a parish pastor.

The Office of Vocation of the Presbyterian Church (USA) asked Roy to complete a research project relating emotional intelligence to effectiveness within an ordained role. They suggested working with three presbyteries within driving distance of Baltimore. The research extended over a six-month period of time. To complete this research, thirty-two people were recruited to take the Hay Group ESCI 360 survey, which includes having up to twenty other people complete the same survey on the individual. Ten of these clergy were to be rated as having high emotional intelligence by their executive presbyter, and ten were to be clergy who were struggling in their pastoral role. To be sure, these were subjective recommendations by these three executive presbyters, but they each had a perspective we valued in this research. They included clergy from New Castle Presbytery, Baltimore Presbytery, and National Capital Union Presbytery. In addition, we were to administer this survey to ten Presbyterian seminarians in a variety of seminaries.

The scores of the seminarians and clergy were to be known only to Roy. Their survey results would be used in this study, but their names were never connected with any EQ score, allowing these people to remain anonymous to their denomination. The resulting report to the Office of Vocation included some interesting insights. Regarding the emotional trait of self-awareness, in the group of clergy rated highly competent, 69 percent showed self-awareness as a strength, whereas only 2 percent of those rated low in competence showed this as a strength. Seminarians fared even better, with 70 percent of them showing self-awareness as a strength.

When clergy rated highly competent were examined, 77 percent showed self-control as a strength, whereas of the group rated low in competence, only 55 percent showed this as a strength. In addition, 9 percent of those scoring low were rated as "rarely" or "never" demonstrating this skill. Seventy percent of seminarians scored high in self-control.

The disparity was even higher when considering the trait of adaptability. Of those rated as competent, 85 percent showed this as a strength, whereas only 27 percent of those rated low showed this as a strength. Seminarians scored high on this in 70 percent of the cases.

How is one able to be competent in congregational ministry without the trait of empathy? Those clergy scoring high in competence showed strength in this trait 85 percent of the time as compared with 36 percent of those scoring low in competence. Seminarians scored 80 percent on this trait.

When measuring skills in conflict management, 85 percent of those clergy rated high in competence showed conflict management as a strength, whereas only 27 percent of those scoring low showed this as a strength. Seminarians came in at 70 percent.

Inspirational leadership is something often sought by congregational leaders. In this summary, 92 percent of those rated as competent in ministry showed this as a strength, whereas only 55 percent of those scoring low showed this as a strength. In addition, 9 percent of those scoring low in competence showed that this was "never" or "rarely" a strength.

The data demonstrated clearly that individuals considered competent by their executive presbyter scored much higher in emotional intelligence than those they saw as struggling in that role.

The transition from layperson to ordained ministry will be a major shift for any individual. This process needs to be managed with care by denominations. Making sure that the right people apply for the ordination track in these denominations has even deeper implications for these judicatories' future viability in the twenty-first century.

Transition from Seminary Culture into One's First Congregation

Some seminaries provide their students with a great environment for learning. Academic inquiry is encouraged. Students can participate in substantive theological debate and biblical research. However, the interpersonal relationships students have with faculty and other students are rarely critiqued or challenged. Moving from this culture to a congregational one can be a real challenge for a newly ordained person. Rather than ability in theological and biblical debate, congregants often want their new pastor to guide them in making the right religious choices—and want them to give their denomination's perspectives on most issues. Interpersonal relationships become central rather than peripheral. The most dramatic shift that takes place in this transition is the movement from being a recipient of care to being thrust into a caregiving leadership role. Rather than having colleagues around to explore issues, the new role can be isolating and lonely. It's a big shift.

Learning a new role is more caught than it is taught. It is something that is learned more by experiencing the projections and expectations of actual members than it is from academic learning. In a pastoral role, newly ordained clergy discover that they are continually engaging in role negotiations with members. How much of the members' projections onto them in their role will the newly ordained clergy accept and wear, and where will they draw the line? Which of those projections will they live into and which will they reject? When newly ordained people are equipped with superior emotional intelligence skills, they will do a better job in managing these projections and surmounting the other challenges of ministry.

The highest clergy drop-out rate is two and a half years out of seminary. Only after men and women have been in the role do they discover they either don't like it or feel they do not have the stamina or the will to continue in that role. Many do not have the emotional intelligence to manage such a complex and changing role.

We will now shift from focusing on clergy to centering on congregational life.

Congregations Involved in a Pastoral Change

From a congregational perspective, managing the transition from one pastor to another involves three distinct steps:

1. Gaining closure with the departing pastor
2. Coping in the interim period, either by calling an interim pastor or by contracting for other professional assistance
3. Welcoming and getting on board with a new pastor

Both the emotional and the spiritual life of a congregation need to be managed well in this transition. The emotional side of congregational life needs to be monitored by lay leaders who focus on keeping the personal and emotional interactions of members in a healthy state. This involves assisting the congregation in dealing with grief and loss, if there is any, and keeping the congregation excited about the new possibilities that can come with calling a new pastor.

We recommend that the congregation appoint a transition committee to give oversight to all the changes the congregation needs to experience in this transition. It is a real challenge to manage a congregation's emotional life through all three of these transitions. A congregation cannot afford to allow a positive congregational climate to degenerate into negativity, boredom, and infighting. While a congregation's governing board continues to manage the fiscal and managerial side of congregational life, a transition committee observes and monitors the emotional tone of the congregation, intervening and making recommendations to the board about ways to keep the congregation upbeat and positive throughout. In small-membership congregations, the governing board may need to do both.

There will be emotional land mines to be maneuvered around if the congregation is to emerge from the departure of a former pastor to the end of the first year of the new pastor with health and vitality. The stages of this transition are described in the book by Roy titled *Beginning Ministry Together.* In summary form, here are a few of them:

1. Terminating a relationship with the outgoing pastor. The transition committee can ask the departing pastor about her plans for saying good-bye to the congregation, keeping her informed about the congregational side of this process, possibly coaching her on people she needs to be sure to contact. Is she allowing enough time for this? How will she sustain positive energy throughout this task? The transition committee can offer to hold an exit conversation with the departing pastor, focusing on her perspective of the congregation she is leaving. What does she perceive needs attention once she has left, and what are the major challenges facing this congregation in the next few years? Such an exit interview can be recorded and shared with the governing board, assisting it in gaining closure with the departing pastor and giving their perspective on what the congregation needs most in the future. A printed copy of this exit interview can also be given to the newly appointed search/call committee as information it can use as it

begins to draft the self-study that the denomination may require before it will suggest potential candidates for the congregation. A sample exit interview questionnaire can be located in the book mentioned above.[5]

The transition committee can also assist in planning farewell events that adequately express the congregation's appreciation for the departing pastor. For longer, positive pastorates, a series of farewell events should be planned, not trying to do it in one event. A congregation will have a hard time inviting in a new pastor when they haven't adequately closed with a former one.

2. Welcome and support for an interim pastor if one is called, or supplying clergy who conduct worship services and offer pastoral care. Seeing to it that an interim pastor has an appropriate job description and pays attention to the emotional needs of the congregation is important. At the conclusion of the interim pastor's service, there should be an evaluation and appropriate closure process with him or her.

3. Having the congregation embrace a new pastor, caring for the emotional needs of the pastor, his children, and his spouse; seeing that there is a positive closure with the search/call committee that called the new pastor; and offering feedback to the new pastor on how the congregation perceives his new ministry will all need to be done.

The tasks and challenges of a congregation going through a pastoral transition are unique to each congregation. Managing this transition is crucial to the future health and vitality of a congregation. A denomination's middle judicatory will no doubt be able to outline the steps that need to be taken in such a transition, but managing the emotional dimensions of each of these stages is a whole other task. We recommend that a congregation consider hiring a transition consultant to work with the transition committee. The congregation can expect that there will be political power moves on the part of some members during this transition. It can also expect to lose some members who see this as a time to renegotiate their relationship with the congregation. Additionally, the congregation can expect some members to be discouraged and in deep grief over the loss of the outgoing pastor. The emotional vulnerability of a congregation facing this pastoral transition can be huge. Some congregations have lost a third to one-half of their members because their transition process was seriously flawed. A congregation can hope that lay leaders with considerable amounts of emotional intelligence will rise to the occasion to lead their congregation through this "dangerous opportunity."

In some ways, what we have offered in this book on the emotional intelligence of Jesus and the need for superior EQ in congregational life are not new. Basically, we have known that congregational life is all about relationships. To be sure, congregations have lost sight of this from time to time. We hope this publication can assist clergy and congregations to remain focused on the importance of this relational intelligence.

Congregations Moving from One Size to Another

Of all the shifts in size, the transition of a congregation from a pastoral-centered congregation to a program-size congregation is the most challenging. Some congregations make many attempts at this size change and simply can't do it successfully. This is mostly due to the shift in the role of the pastor in these two sizes. Members get hooked on having their pastor remain readily available to them when desired. They want to see the pastor at all committee meetings, attending all special occasions, and being in the pulpit every Sunday. They don't mind if this pastor does all the hard work of getting various new programs under way, but "she had better be there for me when I need her." Clergy burn out trying to do both, and in the end they give up. For some congregations, making this transition means having their current pastor resign and having the newly called one focus on program and staff development, giving less attention to individual members' needs. This is tricky, as the new pastor needs to convey the message to members that "if I had time, I would love to get to know you better." It may take three to five years for a congregation to be weaned off receiving all their pastoral care needs from one pastor.

A congregation should not be faulted if it doesn't want to grow from a pastoral-size congregation into a program-size one. It is OK for them to remain a pastoral-size congregation. If the governing body decides it wants to grow numerically into a program-size congregation, they need to know that their pastor may get killed in the process. Once this pastor starts spending most of her time in program development, the complaints are going to be coming to her governing body. "Where is our pastor? How is she spending her time? This is a bad pastor who is never available to us as members." Some clergy die in this ditch or simply receive a call to another congregation because they are burned out and fed up with being thrown under the bus in this attempt at size transition.

One congregation Roy consulted with continued to grow numerically, but when they observed they were getting too large for their facility and the pastor's energy, they spun off a cadre of members to start a new mission congregation down the road. They actually did it twice, founding two new Episcopal congregations in their county. One of those congregations is now triple the size of the founding congregation.

The transition from a family-size congregation to a pastoral-size one may be gradual, but when a small-membership congregation grows numerically and is able to afford a full-time pastor of its own, it will change dramatically. Small-membership congregations usually share a pastor with other congregations in a yoked relationship. The challenge then is to call the right person who has the emotional intelligence to work first with patriarchs or matriarchs in moving the congregation forward and then take over that major leadership role within the congregation.

The transition from program-size to corporate-size takes place as the congregation is able to afford program staff to head up major ministries within the congregation. The congregation needs to adjust to working with staff members rather than with the senior pastor only. The senior pastor needs to shift from working directly with congregants to getting things done by coaching and supervising staff members.

Assimilating New Members: The Transition into Membership

The majority of congregations Roy deals with invest most of their energy in attracting new members and getting them to join. Once the new members have attended a new member's class and have officially joined the congregation, they are often abandoned to find their place within this new spiritual community. From an emotional intelligence perspective, this behavior on the part of congregations does not make sense. Congregations need to have an assimilation process whereby new members are connected to sponsors and their activity within the congregation is monitored throughout their first year of membership. This is especially needed if the congregation requires only one or two new member classes, which means these newcomers do not even get well connected with fellow new members of the class.[6]

The above is not nearly as important if a congregation has in place a six- to nine-month catechumenate process for new members. It is recommended that congregations have two ways a newcomer can join a congregation: an easy one involving one or two new member classes, and a challenging one involving a six- to nine-month catechumenate. Most new members will choose the easy way, especially if they come from another congregation within their denomination. There are some people, however, who feel they have not really been grounded in the basics of the faith and want an in-depth introduction to the faith. Others want the longer process when changing denominations. Congregations with only an easy process for people joining the congregation have little substance to offer new seekers to the faith. They have given up on the 50 percent of the population in North America who have never ever attended a church service or opened the Bible. They expect to grow numerically only by having people transfer to them from other congregations and from other denominations. When a congregation offers only one or two new member classes, it assumes these people know the basics of the faith and they simply need to be oriented to their new congregation.

When a longer orientation for new members is in place, newcomers get exposed to a variety of congregational leaders and the staff, and natural relationships develop. Even in this case, however, each new member should be monitored and coached until he or she has become identified with some social justice ministry of the congregation or one of its internal ministries.

Bringing greater emotional intelligence to the transition moments in the lives of clergy and congregations, as mentioned above, has the potential to bring greater health and wholeness to those involved. It is one concrete way of making congregations more inviting and upgrading the quality of relationships experienced by members. This in turn makes for more attractive communities of faith to outsiders.

The current challenge in congregational life today is that the rate of change in society is continuing to increase. The result is that these transition moments are coming at us at great speed and intensity. It is the intention of this chapter to bring greater awareness of these transition points in ministry, thereby allowing us to be more prepared when they are upon us. This makes for less "danger" when these transitions are upon us and capitalizes on the "opportunities" they bring to us.

Conclusion

Our churches in North America seem to be searching for a deeper spirituality, a lived-out expression of the faith. We see this, for example, in the "new monasticism," which transcends parochial barriers and seeks to inculcate a spirituality for daily life that is modeled on Jesus' life, with less attention to traditional theological claims about Jesus.[7] The fascination with Jesus' life, his character, also shows up in the numerous widely read books about Jesus that seek to locate him in the context of first-century Galilee and of the Roman Empire and to demonstrate the relevance of his teaching both in his day and for today.

The need for a deeper and embodied spirituality may seem especially imperative in a society so deeply and increasingly shaped by the values, attitudes, and ways of living engendered by capitalism and nationalism.[8] Pastors may be frustrated that values and attitudes shaped by capitalism and nationalism are really at the core of their people's identity, rather than the Christian ethos.

We believe that this book offers to churches searching for a deeper spirituality not only a concrete image of what discipleship to Jesus means but also a guide for how this might be inculcated in the congregation. Leaders in our churches need to incarnate a Jesus-shaped form of leadership, and developing their emotional intelligence will equip them to do just that. Pastors probably burn out not just from overwork but also from frustration that their efforts produce so few fruits, that they find themselves unable to find meaning in their work. Developing emotional intelligence skills in pastors, bishops, and other church leaders goes hand in glove with a deepened spirituality. It is really impossible to develop a deeply embodied spirituality without emotional intelligence and the life skills that it entails.

While everyone wants churches to grow, increase giving, and function more smoothly, the real goal of the church experience is an ongoing process of conversion toward a more deeply interiorized, lived-out, compassionate, generous, grateful, and grace-filled Christian life. When this is realized, pastors are energized and congregations are energized. Such congregations matter in the lives of their communities.

It is our hope that this book will point the way toward genuine renewal in our churches. We are not setting forth any surefire formulas for success, but rather some direction toward engendering communities in which a process of genuine conversion can occur, a process that will lead to a deeper embodied spirituality, shaped by Jesus.

Appendix I:
Emotional Traits

In chapter 1, we outlined neuroscientists' current understanding of the relationship between the brain and our intertwined emotional and cognitive processes. Interpreting brain research to the general public is no easy task. We need nonmedical language to help us grasp the workings of our brain. We are especially grateful for the volumes on emotional intelligence produced by Daniel Goleman.[1] Goleman, who is not a neuroscientist but a psychologist, has waded through the continuously unfolding brain research and produced four books on the subject. Most recently there is a growing number of books on the subject that are making this research more accessible to the general public. Richard Davidson—with Sharon Begley, author of *Train Your Mind, Change Your Brain*—has written *The Emotional Life of Your Brain*,[2] bringing this material to us nonscientists in everyday language. (More on Davidson and Begley later.)

Emotional traits are characteristics that authors are using to describe emotional intelligence. They are a set of skills that demonstrate competence in a particular interpersonal, intrapersonal, intragroup, and intergroup function. Intergroup functions are the relationships different groups within a congregation have with each other. Understanding our own traits allows us to identify strengths and weaknesses in our ongoing challenge to lead healthy and productive lives. These traits also allow us to talk about emotional intelligence as specific capacities. They can point us to ways we might become more competent and enjoy significant relationships both inside and outside of work. Specifically, we can identify traits we would like our emotional brain to learn and develop.

We begin with the academic team of John Mayer (University of New Hampshire), Peter Salovey (Yale), and David Caruso (Yale), who developed an emotional intelligence test called the Mayer-Salovey-Caruso Emotional Intelligence Test.[3] Other surveys ask individuals to assess themselves on specific EQ traits, but the MSCEIT approaches emotional intelligence as a set of skills that can be tested. It uses multiple-choice questions to assess respondents' capacity to identify, use, understand, and manage emotions.

The team of psychologist Daniel Goleman (currently at Rutgers University) and psychologist Richard Boyatzis (currently at Case Western Reserve) developed the Emotional and Social Competence Inventory (ESCI, available from Hay Group in Boston, www.haygroup.com). Survey takers are able to assess themselves on twelve EQ traits but can also choose to receive feedback from up to twenty other people on these same traits.

Clinical and organizational psychologist Reuven Bar-On (University of Texas) developed the original Emotional Quotient Inventory (the EQ-i and the EQ-i 360). In 2013, Multi-Health Systems in Toronto revised this work to produce the EQ-i 2.0, which is a revision of the EQ-i. While Dr. Bar-On was not involved in the revision, the EQ-i 2.0 is a product of the continued evolution of emotional intelligence and continues to reflect the essence of the EQ-i and the contributions of Dr. Bar-On. Respondents using this survey self-report on their life and workplace performance in fifteen key areas of emotional skill.

The lists of EQ traits in these separate surveys are not similar, hence the reason for this appendix. We utilize these characteristics in this book, but we are drawing from different authors and difference surveys on emotional intelligence. There are a few traits that several authors have in common, such as the traits of self-awareness and empathy, but for the most part there are few similarities. What follows is an outline of the traits in these four systems. The ones we believe that authors have in common are in italics.

Emotional Style

Given the above four schools of thoughts about emotional traits, we want to delve more deeply into Davidson and Begley's sense of our emotional

ESCI (Hay Group)	EQ-i 2.0 (MHS)	Emotional Style (Davidson)	MSCEIT
Self-Awareness	*Self-Perception*		*Identify/Perceive Emotions*
Emotional Self-Awareness	*Emotional Self-Awareness*	*Awareness Style*	
	Self-Regard		
	Self-Actualization	Attention Style	
Self-Management	*Self-Expression*		Using Emotions
Achievement Orientation	Emotional Expression		
Adaptability	Assertiveness	Resilience	
Emotional Self-Control	*Impulse Control*		
Positive Outlook	*Optimism*	*Outlook Style*	
Social Awareness			
	Interpersonal		
Empathy	*Empathy*		
Organizational Awareness	Interpersonal Relationships		Understanding Emotions
	Social Responsibility		
Relationship Management	Decision Making		
Conflict Management	Problem Solving	Social Intuition Style	
Coach and Mentor	Reality Testing		
Influence	Impulse Control		Managing Emotions
Inspirational Leadership	Stress Management		
Teamwork	Flexibility		Sensitivity to Context
	Stress Tolerance		

style. These two authors stand apart from the others in that their six emotional styles can all be backed by concrete scientific data on the brain. For example, you may have the opportunity to measure your resilience style in a survey, but Davidson can hook you up to an fMRI (functional magnetic resonance imaging) and tell you about your specific resilience style. This would not be true for the other authors who have developed their own set of emotional traits.

Davidson and Begley begin their book by summarizing the evolution of research measuring emotions in the brain. When Davidson began studying psychology in the 1970s, emotions were considered merely "static" or "disruption" that got in the way of important mental processes. The ascendant style of therapy was cognitive psychology—straighten out the way people think, therapists believed, and you can change the way they feel and act. While Davidson continued his postgraduate studies, scientists were developing ways to measure brain activities. They were able to place electrodes on people's heads that enabled the scientists to determine which parts of the brain were being activated when the person was asked to perform certain tasks; this in turn enabled the scientists to produce an electroencephalogram (EEG), a record of that activity.

In 1989, when Davidson was reviewing research data on the prefrontal lobes, he developed his theory of "emotional styles"—"constellations of emotional reactions and coping responses that differ in kind, intensity, and duration."[4] He observed that people engaged the right prefrontal lobe of the brain when they viewed film clips that provoked fright or disgust (i.e., negative emotions), and the left prefrontal lobe registered activity when they viewed uplifting film clips (positive emotions). He also noticed that the strength of these impulses differed from individual to individual. What emerged were six different emotional styles that could be measured via by EEG or, later, fMRI. In other words, he found that neuroscientists did not need to ask people if their outlook on life was more positive than negative; the neuroscientists could measure their brain activity and tell. They didn't need to ask people if they believed they could discern the behavior appropriate in various social contexts; the MRI would answer that question for them. It is unlikely that people will admit they lack self-awareness, but a scan of their brain can tell the extent to which people are aware of thoughts and feelings or simply acting or reacting without knowing why. A brain scan can also indicate whether people are socially intuitive or mainly puzzled by other people. Likewise, a brain scan can tell whether a person recovers quickly from setback or trauma or has a meltdown after experiencing adversity.

Davidson was impressed with how plastic the human brain is. He found that people could change their emotional style by conscious thought and activity. He was particularly impressed with how certain forms of meditation can change one's emotional style, which involves actually altering the physical structure of one's brain by means of thought alone. One of the distinctive qualities of Davidson's work, and, indeed, the work of many neuroscientists, is that it does not focus on pathological conditions (mental diseases) but on what makes for healthy living. In fact, Davidson is director of the Laboratory for Affective Neuroscience and the Center for Investigating Healthy Minds, both at the University of Wisconsin–Madison. This focus on healthy emotions lends itself especially well to the cultivation of emotional intelligence.

Each emotional style identified by Davidson is associated with different specific, identifiable brain circuits. For each style, there is a continuum from very strong evidence of the style to very weak evidence (size of that portion of the brain), pointing to either a strength or a challenge to a certain individual's brain. It should be noted that not only do people fall into various locations along each continuum, on a scale of one to ten on each extreme, but there is also not necessarily a "right" location for any particular individual (though, in most cases, being at one or the other extreme end of a spectrum will result in relational difficulties). Davidson explains that the combination of an individual's positions on all six dimensions adds up the person's emotional style.[5] Davidson says humans experience fleeting emotional *states* and longer lasting *moods*, but an emotional *style* is "a consistent way of responding to the experiences of our lives."[6]

Appendix II: Clergy Life Changes Rating Scale*

T he following Life Changes Rating Scale was adapted by Roy M. Oswald from the Holmes/Rahe Scale and field-tested with clergy groups from various denominations.

Strong scientific evidence indicates that the more social readjustments individuals make, the greater their chances of future significant health changes.[1] The severity of health change also tends to increase the score even more.

Since each individual's tolerance for stress varies, the total life changes score should be taken as a rough guide. For each of the events below that you consider yourself to have experienced during the past twelve months, transfer the "average value" to the line in the "your score" column. Add these for your total life changes score.

---

* This material can be found in an extended form in the following two books: Roy M. Oswald, *Clergy Self Care* (Herndon, VA: Alban Institute, 1991); and Roy M. Oswald, James Heath, and Ann Heath, *Beginning Ministry Together: The Alban Handbook on Clergy Transitions* (Herndon, VA: Alban Institute, 2003).

Clergy Life Changes Rating Scale

Event	Average Value	Your Score
Death of a spouse	100	
Divorce	73	
Marital separation	65	
Death of a close family member	63	
Personal injury or illness	53	
Marriage	50	
Serious decline in church attendance	49	
Geographical relocation	49	
Private meetings by segment of congregation to discuss your resignation	47	
Beginning of heavy drinking by immediate family member	46	
Marital reconciliation	45	
Retirement	45	
Change in health of a family member	44	
Problem with children	42	
Pregnancy	40	
Sex difficulties	39	
Alienation from one's board/council/session/vestry	39	
Gain of new family member	39	
New job in new line of work	38	
Change of financial state	38	
Death of a close friend	37	
Increased arguing with spouse	35	
Troubled child in school	35	
Merger of two or more congregations	35	
Serious parish financial difficulty	32	

Event	Average Value	Your Score
Mortgage over $150,000 for home	31	
Difficulty with member of church staff (associates, organist, choir director, secretary, janitor, etc.)	31	
Difficulty finding adequate child care	30	
Destruction of church by fire	30	
New job in same line of work	30	
Son or daughter leaving home	29	
Trouble with in-laws	29	
Anger of influential church member over pastor's action	29	
Slow, steady decline in church attendance	29	
Outstanding personal achievement	28	
Introduction of new hymnal to worship service	28	
Failure of church to make payroll	27	
Remodeling or building program	27	
Start or stop of spouse's employment	26	
Holiday away	26	
Start or finish of school	26	
Death of peer	26	
Offer of call to another parish	26	
Change in living conditions	25	
Revision of personal habits	24	
Negative parish activity by former pastor	24	
Difficulty with confirmation class	22	
Change in residence	20	
Change in schools	20	
Change in recreation	19	
Change in social activities	18	

Event	Average Value	Your Score
Death/moving away of good church leader	18	
Mortgage or personal loan of less than $150,000	17	
Change in sleeping habits	16	
Development of new friendships	16	
Change in eating habits	15	
Stressful continuing education experience	15	
Major program change	15	
Vacation at home	13	
Christmas	12	
Lent	12	
Easter	12	
Minor violation of the law	11	
Your Total		

Since everyone handles life changes and stress differently, we are not able to cite specific numbers that indicate your level of stress. We do know, however, that whenever an individual passes a certain threshold level of stress, he or she will experience some form of physical malaise or illness. Since everyone's threshold level of stress is different, we refer you to appendix III, which contains the Strain Response Inventory. This second survey will let you know whether you have crossed your threshold level of stress.

As a generalization, however, here are some life changes scores that relate these two surveys with one another.

Life Changes Scores of 100 or less

Few symptoms of stress
Possibly too little stress in one's life, with too few challenges

Life Changes Scores of 101 to 200

Some symptoms of stress appearing
We might call it creative stress

Life Changes Scores of 201 to 300

More symptoms of stress appearing
One is possibly over the top of one's threshold level of stress
Self-care strategies need to be engaged if further illness is to be avoided

Appendix III: The Strain Response Inventory

The material below is adapted from John D. Adams's survey "The Strain Response." It is used here with permission of the author.

The Strain Response Inventory is another way to measure whether you are living your life below, above, or just at your stress threshold. Stress that is no longer productive for us usually results in some sort of strain on our lives.

0 = Never
1 = Infrequently
2 = Frequently
3 = Regularly

Strain Rating	#	Strain Inventory
_____	1	Eat too much
_____	2	Drink too much alcohol
_____	3	Smoke more than usual
_____	4	Feel tense, uptight, fidgety
_____	5	Feel depressed or remorseful
_____	6	Like myself less
_____	7	Have difficulty going to sleep or staying asleep
_____	8	Feel restless and unable to concentrate
_____	9	Have decreased interest in sex
_____	10	Have increased interest in sex
_____	11	Have loss of appetite
_____	12	Feel tired/low energy
_____	13	Feel irritable
_____	14	Think about suicide
_____	15	Become less communicative
_____	16	Feel disoriented or overwhelmed
_____	17	Have difficulty getting up in the morning
_____	18	Have headaches
_____	19	Have upset stomach
_____	20	Have sweaty and/or trembling hands
_____	21	Have shortness of breath and sighing
_____	22	Let things slide
_____	23	Misdirected anger
_____	24	Feel "unhealthy"
_____	25	Feel time bound, anxious about too much to do in too little time
_____	26	Use prescription drugs to relax
_____	27	Use medication for high blood pressure
_____	28	Depend on recreational drugs to relax
_____	29	Have anxiety about the future
_____	30	Have back problems
_____	31	Unable to clear up a cold, running nose, sore throat, cough, infection
_____		**Total Score (add all your numbers)**

Interpreting Your Score

0-20

Below-average strain in your life.

21-30

Stress starting to show its effects in your life. You are living life near your stress threshold, at times crossing it.

31-40

Above-average strain. Stress is having a very destructive effect on your life. You are living a good portion of your life beyond your stress threshold.

40+

Unless you do something soon to alleviate your stress, more serious illness will follow.

Notes

Prologue

1. Daniel Goleman, *Social Intelligence: The New Science of Human Relationships* (New York: Bantam Dell, 2007), 3–4. Goleman's account was based on a report on *All Things Considered*, National Public Radio, April 4, 2003.
2. All quotations from Scripture in this book are from the *New Revised Standard Version Bible*, copyright 1989, Division of Christian Education of the National Council of the Churches of Christ in the United States of America.
3. See Leviticus 20:10 and Deuteronomy 22:22.
4. The NRSV notes that other ancient manuscripts read "him" instead of "them."

Chapter 1

1. John D. Mayer and Peter Salovey, "Emotional Intelligence," in *Imagination, Cognition, and Personality* 6 (1990), 185–211. For a comparison of "Models of Emotional Intelligence," see the article of that title by John D. Mayer, Peter Salovey, and David Caruso in *Handbook of Intelligence*, ed. Robert J. Sternberg (Cambridge: Cambridge University Press, 2000), 396–420. See also Pablo Fernández-Berrocal and Natalio Extremera, "Emotional Intelligence: A Theoretical and Empirical Review of Its First 15 Years," *Psicothema* 18 (2006): 7–12.

2. Goleman, *Emotional Intelligence* (New York: Bantam, 1995). See also his *Primal Leadership: Realizing the Power of Emotional Intelligence* (Cambridge, MA: Harvard Business School Press, 2002), coauthored with Richard Boyatzis and Annie McKee; *Social Intelligence: The New Science of Human Relationships* (New York: Bantam, 2006); and *The Brain and Emotional Intelligence: New Insights* (Northampton, MA: More Than Sound, 2011).

3. *Time*, October 2, 1995. The cover reads, "What's Your EQ?"

4. Mayer and Salovey, "Emotional Intelligence," 189.

5. This list is from Goleman, *Emotional Intelligence*, 43.

6. Daniel Goleman and Richard Boyatzis, "Emotional and Social Competency Inventory," the Hay Group, 2012, http://www.haygroup.com/leadershipand-talentondemand/ourproducts/item_details.aspx?itemid=58&type=1.

7. Multi-Health Systems is an international company that provides a number of professional assessment tools. The list is from the *360 Feedback Report* generated by MHS (Toronto: Multi-Health Systems, 2011). This survey requires rating by fifteen to twenty individuals who have some association with the individual being assessed.

8. Some examples that we have found helpful are David Eagleman, *Incognito: The Secret Lives of the Brain* (New York: Vintage, 2011), Amazon's Best Book of 2011; Richard Davidson and Sharon Begley, *The Emotional Life of Your Brain* (New York: Hudson Street, 2012), a *New York Times* bestseller; Tali Sharot, *The Optimism Bias: A Tour of the Irrationally Positive Brain* (New York: Pantheon, 2011); and Elaine Fox, *Rainy Brain, Sunny Brain: How to Retrain Your Brain to Overcome Pessimism and Achieve a More Positive Outlook* (New York: Basic, 2012).

9. Daniel Goleman, "Emotional Intelligence: Issues in Paradigm Building," in *The Emotionally Intelligent Workplace*, ed. Cary Cherniss and Daniel Goleman (San Francisco: Jossey-Bass, 2001), 23.

10. This case is in Goleman, *Emotional Intelligence*, 35. The results of the first decade of the "Illinois Valedictorian Project" were reported by Karen Arnold, *Academic Achievement—A View from the Top: The Illinois Valedictorian Project* (Oak Grove, IL: North Central Regional Education Laboratory, 1993), 76 pages.

11. Goleman, *Emotional Intelligence*, 36.

12. See, for example, Vanessa Urch Druskat, Fabio Sala, and Gerald Mount, eds., *Linking Emotional Intelligence and Performance at Work: Current Research Evidence with Individuals and Groups* (Mahwah, NJ: Erlbaum, 2006).

13. See Reuven Bar-On, Richard Handley, and Suzanne Fund, "The Impact of Emotional Intelligence on Performance," in *Linking Emotional Intelligence and Performance at Work*, ed. Vanessa Urch Druskat, Fabio Sala, and Gerald Mount (Mahwah, NJ: Erlbaum, 2006), 3–19. See also Reuven Bar-On, "Preliminary Report: A New US Air Force Study Explores the Cost-Effectiveness

of Applying the Bar-On EQ-I," *Emotional Intelligence Insider Report*, August 2010, www.mhs.com.

14. Especially important for our purposes is William James's seminal essay, "What Is an Emotion?" *Mind* 9 (1884): 188–205. James's theory that feelings are the interpretation of bodily events related to emotions remains influential.

15. The full account of this man and the numerous tests to which he was subjected is in Antonio Damasio, *Descartes' Error: Emotion, Reason, and the Human Brain* (New York: Penguin Books, 2005; first published in New York by G. P. Putnam's Sons, 1994), chapter 3. Damasio, a neuroscientist at the University of Iowa Medical Center at the time, was asked to examine the man.

16. Damasio, *Descartes' Error*, 159 (his emphasis).

17. "'I think historically the subject was thought to be very simple: that brain neurons were lost from birth onwards,' explains Caleb Finch, Ph.D., the ARCO/William F. Kieschnick Chair in the Neurobiology of Aging and a professor of gerontology and biological sciences. 'Now it is really clear that if you don't have a specific disease that causes loss of nerve cells, then most, if not all, of the neurons remain healthy until you die. That's a big change, and it has only come about in the last 10 years.'" Quoted in Monika Guttman, "The Aging Brain," *USC Health Magazine*, Spring 2001, https://news.usc.edu/7569/The-Aging-Brain/.

18. Norman Doidge, *The Brain That Changes Itself: Stories of Personal Triumph from the Frontiers of Brain Science* (New York: Viking Penguin, 2007).

19. Maryanne Wolf, *Proust and the Squid: The Story and Science of the Reading Brain* (New York: HarperCollins, 2007), 5.

Chapter 2

1. We accept the most common assumptions about the first three (or "synoptic") Gospels—namely, that Mark was the earliest, and that Matthew and Luke both used Mark, plus a very old additional source usually called simply "Q," in addition to some other sources. Because John's Gospel is of a quite different character and is generally regarded as less valuable as a historical source, though parts of it have historical value, we draw primarily on the synoptic Gospels.

2. Published in German in 1913, this short study, translated by Charles R. Joy, was published in English in 1948 and republished in 1975 by Peter Smith Publisher (Gloucester, MA).

3. This is a pattern that would continue when Palestine became a center of early monasticism. For example, Cyril of Scythopolis reports that a monk named Euthymius gained a reputation for his miraculous healings, and that after healing a boy, Terebôn, he was so besieged with people seeking to be cured that his solitary lifestyle was disturbed. Cyril of Scythopolis, *The Lives of the*

Monks of Palestine, trans. R. M. Price (Kalamazoo, MI: Cistercian, 1991), 14–17.

4. In *Jesus the Jew: A Historian's Reading of the Gospels* (London: William Collins Sons, 1973), Geza Vermes placed Jesus in the context of first-century Galilean "charismatic Judaism," which included healing and other miracle working, meaning he would have been seen as a holy man. While it is possible to question whether his sources—all much later—pertain exactly to the first century, his work has gained quite wide acceptance. A very sophisticated and persuasive approach to Jesus as shaman has been argued by Pieter F. Craffert, *The Life of a Galilean Shaman: Jesus of Nazareth in Anthropological-Historical Perspective* (Eugene, OR: Cascade Books, 2008). Our discussion of Jesus as a healer has been aided by Craffert's work.

5. See Robert W. Funk et al., eds., *The Acts of Jesus: The Search for the Authentic Deeds of Jesus* (San Francisco: HarperSanFrancisco, 1998), 59–60, 530–31.

6. These developments are carefully developed by Jonathan L. Reed in *Archaeology and the Galilean Jesus: A Re-examination of the Evidence* (Harrisburg, PA: Trinity Press International, 2000), 62–99. See also Richard A. Horsley, *Galilee: History, Politics, People* (Valley Forge, PA: Trinity Press International, 1995), 218–20, and Douglas E. Oakman, *Jesus and the Peasants* (Eugene, OR: Cascade Books, 2008).

7. See Exodus 15:26, Psalm 103:3, and Sirach 38:1–5, especially vv. 1–2.

8. For more details regarding her social isolation as well as her restoration to community, see Stuart L. Love, "Jesus Heals the Hemorrhaging Woman," in *The Social Setting of Jesus and the Gospels*, ed. Wolfgang Stegemann, Bruce J. Malina, and Gerd Theissen (Minneapolis: Augsburg Fortress, 2002), 85–101.

9. John Pilch, *Healing in the New Testament: Insights from Medical and Mediterranean Anthropology* (Minneapolis: Fortress, 2000). Other pioneers are Stevan Davies, *Jesus the Healer: Possession, Trance, and the Origins of Christianity* (New York: Continuum, 1995), and Santiago Guijarro, "Healing Stories and Medical Anthropology: A Reading of Mark 10:46–52," *Biblical Theology Bulletin* 30, no. 3 (2000): 102–12.

10. Guijarro, "Healing Stories," 103.

11. See Craffert, *Life of a Galilean Shaman*, chapter 9.

12. This leprosy is not to be identified with the kind of leprosy that causes parts of the body to fall off. See, for example, Max Sussman, "Diseases in the Bible and Talmud," in *Diseases in Antiquity*, ed. Don Brothwell and A. T. Sandison (Springfield, IL: Charles C. Thomas, 1967), esp. 216–17. A more recent examination is by Joel S. Baden and Candida R. Moss, "The Origin and Interpretation of *ṣāraʿat* in Leviticus 13–14," *Journal of Biblical Literature* 130, no. 4 (Winter 2011): 643–62 (*ṣāraʿat* is translated as "leprosy" in the Old Testament).

13. Davies, *Jesus the Healer*.

14. For this change in terminology, see American Psychiatric Association, "Somatic Symptom Disorder," dsm5.org, http://www.dsm5.org/Documents/Somatic%20 Symptom%20Disorder%20Fact%20Sheet.pdf.

15. Craffert, *Life of a Galilean Shaman*, 285–86. Craffert also understands the illnesses Jesus healed as somatic disorders.

16. Craffert, *Life of a Galilean Shaman*, 285.

17. Donald Capps, *Jesus the Village Psychiatrist* (Louisville, KY: Westminster John Knox Press, 2008). See especially chapter 7, "Jairus' Daughter and the Hemorrhaging Woman." Capps seems unaware of Davies's earlier work.

18. George M. Foster, "Peasant Society and the Image of Limited Good," *American Anthropologist* 67, no. 2 (April 1965): 293–315.

19. "Peasant Society and the Image of Limited Good," 296; his emphasis.

20. "Peasant Society and the Image of Limited Good," 297.

21. Sendhil Mullainathan and Eldar Shafir, *Scarcity: Why Having Too Little Means So Much* (New York: Times Books, 2013).

22. For the absence of elite structures in Capernaum, see Reed, *Archaeology and the Galilean Jesus*, chapter 5, especially pp. 164–68. Also see Reed's chapter, "Archaeological Contributions to the Study of Jesus and the Gospels," in *The Historical Jesus in Context*, ed. Amy-Jill Levine, Dale C. Allison Jr., and John Dominic Crossan (Princeton, NJ: Princeton University Press, 2006).

23. For the economic situation in Jesus' Galilee, see Oakman, *Jesus and the Peasants*, especially part 1, "Political Economy and the Peasant Values of Jesus."

24. For subsistence fishing, see K. C. Hanson and Douglas E. Oakman, *Palestine in the Time of Jesus: Social Structures and Social Conflicts* (Minneapolis: Fortress, 1998), especially pp. 106–10.

25. See Shelley Wachsmann, *The Sea of Galilee Boat: A 2000-Year-Old Discovery from the Sea of Legends* (Cambridge, MA: Perseus, 1995, 2000).

26. Crossan's groundbreaking book is *In Parables: The Challenge of the Historical Jesus* (New York: Harper & Row, 1973). Crossan has revisited parables recently in *The Power of Parable: How Fiction by Jesus Became Fiction about Jesus* (New York: HarperCollins, 2012).

27. See, for example, Walter Brueggemann, "The Liturgy of Abundance, the Myth of Scarcity," *Christian Century*, March 24–31, 1999, and "Enough Is Enough," *Other Side* 37, no. 5 (November–December 2001). "The Liturgy of Abundance" was reprinted in Walter Brueggemann, *Deep Memory, Exuberant Hope: Contested Truth in a Post-Christian World*, ed. Patrick D. Miller (Minneapolis: Augsburg Fortress, 2000), 69–76.

28. We are following the view most clearly expressed in the three synoptic Gospels, though also in the Fourth Gospel.

29. The Greek word translated "fully qualified" (*katartidzo*) means fully trained, made complete, perfected.

Chapter 3

1. For the report on this research, go to http://www.haygroup.com/downloads/ ww/misc/esci_research_findings_2010.pdf.
2. The case is described in Antonio Damasio, *Descartes' Error: Emotion, Reason, and the Human Brain* (New York: Penguin, 1994), chapter 3.
3. Bstan-'dzin-rgya-mtsho, Dalai Lama XIV, *The Essence of Happiness: A Guidebook for Living*, edited by Howard C. Cutler (New York: Riverhead Books, 2010), and *The Pocket Dalai Lama*, compiled and edited by Mary Craig (Boston: Shambhala, 2002).
4. Daniel Goleman, narrator, *Destructive Emotions: How Can We Overcome Them? A Scientific Dialogue with the Dalai Lama* (New York: Bantam, 2003).
5. These weeklong workshops are offered by the Center for EQ-HR Skills, which focuses its ministry on clergy, seminarians, and religious leaders: www.eqhrcenter.org.
6. The classic collection is Helen Waddell's *The Desert Fathers* (Ann Arbor: University of Michigan Press, 1957; first published by Constable, 1936). This has been supplemented more recently by Laura Swan's *The Forgotten Desert Mothers: Sayings, Lives and Stories of Early Christian Women* (Mahwah, NJ: Paulist, 2001). The appropriation of the Bible by desert monks has been explored by Douglas Burton-Christie, *The Word in the Desert: Scripture and the Quest for Holiness in Early Christian Monasticism* (New York: Oxford University Press, 1993).
7. See, for example, Pierre Hadot, *Philosophy as a Way of Life: Spiritual Exercises from Socrates to Foucault*, trans. Michael Chase, ed. and with an introduction by Arnold I. Davidson (Malden, MA: Blackwell, 1995).

Chapter 4

1. Daniel Goleman, *Social Intelligence* (New York: Bantam Dell, 2005), 58; his emphasis.
2. Marco Iacoboni, *Mirroring People: The Science of Empathy and How We Connect with Others* (New York: Picador, 2009).
3. Iacoboni, *Mirroring People*, 9.
4. Iacoboni, *Mirroring People*, 34.
5. Iacoboni, *Mirroring People*, 268.
6. Simon Baron-Cohen, *The Science of Evil: On Empathy and the Origins of Cruelty* (New York: Basic, 2011), 28.
7. Baron-Cohen, *Science of Evil*. See chapter 2, "The Empathy Mechanism: The Bell Curve," especially his description of "the empathy circuit" (pp. 27–41).

8. For extended discussion of this, see James Blair, Derek Mitchell, and Karina Blair, *The Psychopath: Emotion and the Brain* (London: Blackwell, 2005).
9. Daniel Goleman, *Emotional Intelligence* (New York: Bantam, 1995), 96.
10. Goleman, *Emotional Intelligence*, 97.
11. Goleman, *Emotional Intelligence*, 97.
12. Paul Ekman and Wallace Friesen, *Unmasking the Face: A Guide to Recognizing Emotions from Facial Expressions* (Englewood Cliffs, NJ: Prentice Hall, 1975). Ekman has written other, more recent, books, including *Emotions Revealed: Recognizing Faces and Feelings to Improve Communication and Emotional Life* (New York: Times Books, 2003; 2nd ed., Holt Paperbacks, 2007). Ekman begins the latter by telling the story of how the universality of facial expressions was discovered.
13. For more information and for a review of research on this, see David Matsumoto, Dacher Keltner, Michelle N. Shiota, Maureen O'Sullivan, and Mark Frank, "Facial Expression of Emotions," in *Handbook of Emotions*, 3rd ed., ed. Michael Lewis, Jeannette M. Haviland-Jones, and Lisa Feldman Barrett (New York: Guilford, 2008), 211–34.
14. G. Brent Darnell, *The People-Profit Connection: How Emotional Intelligence Can Maximize People Skills and Maximize Your Profits*, 3rd ed. (Atlanta: BDI, 2011). The second edition of his CD recording of the book may be obtained at www.brentdarnell.com.
15. Goleman, *Social Intelligence*, 59.
16. Martha C. Nussbaum, *The New Religious Intolerance* (Cambridge, MA: Belknap Press of Harvard University, 2012).
17. For more information about the Center for EQ-HR Skills, go to their website: www.EQHRCenter.org.
18. The *Oxford English Dictionary* says it was created in the early twentieth century.
19. The word occurs in Mark 1:41; 6:34 (Matthew 14:14; cf. Matthew 9:36); Mark 8:2 (Matthew 15:32); Mark 9:22; Matthew 18:27; 20:34; Luke 7:13; 10:33; 15:20. The writers of the Gospels seem to clearly distinguish this "compassion" from "mercy" (*eleos*, usually referring to acts of divine mercy), and consistently use the related verb *eleeō* for the numerous cries to Jesus to "have mercy."
20. See Helmut Koester, *Theological Dictionary of the New Testament*, vol. 7 (Grand Rapids, MI: Eerdmans, 1971), 548–59.
21. For example, a blind man (Mark 10:47–48), a Canaanite woman (Matthew 15:22), the father of an epileptic (Matthew 17:15), the rich man in Hades (Luke 16:24), and lepers (Luke 17:13).
22. Hans Dieter Betz, *Essays on the Sermon on the Mount* (Philadelphia: Fortress, 1985), 5.

Chapter 5

1. Edwin H. Friedman, *A Failure of Nerve* (New York: Seabury, 1999, 2007).
2. Daniel Ames and Francis Flynn, "What Breaks a Leader: The Curvilinear Relation between Assertiveness and Leadership," *Journal of Personality and Social Psychology* 92, no. 2 (2007): 307.
3. Probably the word that comes closest to "assertive" is *parrāsia* [παρρησια], which can mean openness, boldness, confidence. In its only occurrence in the synoptics, Jesus tells the disciples "openly" about what must happen to the Son of Man (Mark 8:32). Paul speaks of "boldness" (e.g., 2 Corinthians 3:12).
4. For the argument that the controversy dialogues are later church views attributed to Jesus, see Rudolf Bultmann, *The History of the Synoptic Tradition*, trans. John Marsh (New York: Harper & Row, 1963), 39–41.

Chapter 6

1. Both Reuven Bar-On (developer of the EQ-360 survey, copyrighted in 2011 by Multi-Health Systems Inc.) and Daniel Goleman and Richard Boyatzis (developers of the Emotional and Social Competency Inventory, copyrighted by the Hay Group in Boston) place optimism high on their rating scales of EQ.
2. Martin Seligman, *Learned Optimism: How to Change Your Mind and Life* (New York: Free Press, 1998).
3. Richard J. Davidson with Sharon Begley, *The Emotional Life of Your Brain* (New York: Hudson Street, 2012), 48–50. For the use of mindfulness training to affect outlook, see 200–205.
4. Elaine Fox, *Rainy Brain, Sunny Brain* (New York: Basic, 2012), 48.
5. Fox, *Rainy Brain, Sunny Brain*, 34.
6. Fox, *Rainy Brain, Sunny Brain*, 40.
7. Fox, *Rainy Brain, Sunny Brain*, 41.
8. Fox, *Rainy Brain, Sunny Brain*, 78.
9. Fox, *Rainy Brain, Sunny Brain*, 79.
10. Mark 6:30–44/Matthew 14:13–21/Luke 9:10–17/John 6:1–13, and Mark 8:1–10/Matthew 15:32–39.

Chapter 7

1. Thomas Holmes and Richard Rahe, "The Social Readjustment Rating Scale," *Journal of Psychosomatic Research* 11, no. 2 (1967): 213–18.
2. John D. Adams, the Strain Response Inventory, shared with Roy in a consultation, copy in appendix III.

3. See Bruce M. Metzger, *A Textual Commentary on the Greek New Testament* (London: United Bible Societies, 1971), 177, for details.
4. *Lutheran Book of Worship* (Minneapolis: Augsburg Fortress, 1978), 153.

Chapter 8

1. Paul also reflects Jesus' thoughts in Romans 12:14–21.
2. See, for example, Evelin Lindner, *Making Enemies: Humiliation and International Conflict* (Westport, CT: Praeger Security International, 2006), and Thomas J. Scheff, *Bloody Revenge: Emotions, Nationalism and War* (Lincoln, NE: An Authors Guild Backprint, 2000; originally published in 1994).
3. David Lacey, "The Role of Humiliation in the Palestinian/Israeli Conflict in Gaza," *Psychology and Society* 4, no. 1 (2011): 76–92.
4. See, for example, Peter Bergen and Michael Lind, "A Matter of Pride," *Democracy: A Journal of Ideas*, no. 3 (Winter 2007): 8–16. The authors rely in part on the study by Robert A. Pape, *Dying to Win: The Strategic Logic of Suicide Terrorism* (New York: Random House, 2006), which discounts causes such as poverty and Islamic fundamentalism and focuses on the humiliation of foreign military occupation.
5. Bettina Muenster and David Lotto, "The Social Psychology of Humiliation and Revenge: The Origins of the Fundamentalist Mindset," in *The Fundamentalist Mindset: Psychological Perspectives on Religion, Violence, and History*, ed. Charles B. Strozier, David M. Terman, and James W. Jones, with Katharine A. Boyd (Oxford: Oxford University Press, 2010), 71–79.
6. Zheng Wang, *Never Forget National Humiliation: Historical Memory in Chinese Politics and Foreign Relations* (New York: Columbia University Press, 2012).
7. See Walter Wink's article, "Neither Passivity nor Violence: Jesus' Third Way (Matt. 5:38–42 par.)," in *The Love of Enemy and Nonretaliation in the New Testament*, ed. Willard M. Swartley (Louisville, KY: Westminster John Knox, 1992), 102–25.
8. See Douglas E. Oakman, "Jesus and the Problem of Debt in Ancient Palestine," in *Jesus and the Peasants* (Eugene, OR: Cascade Books, 2008), 33–39.
9. For the rule about demanding payment of a debt, see Deuteronomy 24:10–13.
10. The Greek word to "force" someone (*aggareuo*) used here refers to a widespread practice in the Greco-Roman world of compulsory labor for the state (known by its Latin equivalent, *angareiae*), which was by no means limited to soldiers. Simon of Cyrene was "compelled" to carry Jesus' cross (Mark 15:21). For this practice, see M. Rostovtzeff, *Social and Economic History of the Roman Empire*, vol. 1 (Oxford: Oxford University Press, 1926), 380–85.

11. On Paul's odd "heap coals on the head" as the outcome of caring for the enemy, see Robert Jewett, *Romans: A Commentary* (Minneapolis: Fortress, 2007), 777. It probably means to win over the enemy.
12. Muenster and Lotto, "Social Psychology of Humiliation," 71.
13. Muenster and Lotto, "Social Psychology of Humiliation," 72.
14. N. R. Kleinfield, Ray Rivera, and Serge F. Kovaleski, "Newtown Killer's Obsessions, in Chilling Detail," *New York Times*, March 28, 2013.
15. There is a study of this theme by Klaus Wengst, *Humility: Solidarity of the Humiliated* (Philadelphia: Fortress, 1988).
16. See, for example, Erica Chenoweth and Maria J. Stephan, *Why Civil Resistance Works: The Strategic Logic of Nonviolent Conflict* (New York: Columbia University Press, 2011). The authors demonstrate that nonviolent resistance has been far more effective, in both the short term and especially the long term, than violent resistance.
17. Maxine Kaufman-Lacusta, *Refusing to Be Enemies: Palestinian and Israeli Nonviolent Resistance to the Israeli Occupation*, with a foreword by Ursula Franklin (Reading, UK: Ithaca, 2011).
18. Izzeldin Abuelaish, *I Shall Not Hate: A Gaza Doctor's Journey on the Road to Peace and Human Dignity* (New York: Walker, 2011).
19. Izzeldin Abuelaish, interview by Rachel Cooke, *Guardian/Observer*, January 16, 2011.
20. Mazim Qumsiyeh, *Popular Resistance in Palestine: A History of Hope and Empowerment* (New York: Pluto Press, 2010).

Chapter 9

1. For the full story, see Donald B. Kraybill, Steven M. Nolt, and David L. Weaver-Zercher, *Amish Grace: How Forgiveness Transcended Tragedy* (San Francisco: Jossey-Bass, 2007).
2. Forgiveness and forgiving are frequently mentioned in the Old Testament, but almost exclusively God is the forgiver. Only a few instances of interpersonal forgiveness can be found there: Genesis 50:17, Exodus 10:17, and 1 Samuel 15:25 and 25:28, where individuals request forgiveness for wrongs done to them by offenders. There is a single reference to interpersonal forgiveness in the Apocrypha/Deuterocanonical books—namely, Sirach 28:2 ("Forgive your neighbor the wrong he has done, and then your sins will be pardoned when you pray"). This notion of reciprocal forgiveness is similar to some of Jesus' sayings (e.g., Matthew 6:14–15; Mark 11:25; Luke 6:37). Similar sayings are found in the Pseudepigrapha and other Jewish writings (see Patrick W. Skehan and Alexander A. DiLella, *The Wisdom of Ben Sira* [New York: Anchor Bible, 1987], 363–64).
3. This is the NRSV translation. The Greek is the neuter *teknon*, meaning child, of indeterminate gender.

4. The inclusive plural *anthropoi* is used.

5. We take the more radical view in Matthew as definitive on the same principle used in textual criticism, that the harder reading is generally preferable; here, "harder" or more difficult is the more radical of the versions of Jesus' sayings. It is easier to explain the softening of a text than its hardening because the tendency in the tradition is generally to take the hard edges off texts.

6. Ulrich Luz also sees the likely connection between these texts, and says that Jesus is calling for the complete abolition of revenge, which, he shows, has troubled the churches down through history so much that they have largely ignored it (Ulrich Luz, *Matthew 8–20* [Minneapolis: Fortress, 2001], 465–66).

7. This is sometimes explicit (e.g., Proverbs 20:22; 24:29; 25:21–22), but there are also many admonitions to restrain anger because it stirs up strife (e.g., Proverbs 3:27–32; 10:12; 11:12; 15:18; 16:32; 24:17–18; 29:11; 30:33). The command to love the neighbor, in fact, is prefaced by the prohibition of personal revenge and the bearing of grudges (Leviticus 19:18).

8. For example, Luz thinks the text originated in a Jewish Christian community: in Matthew 18:17, "Gentile" is still a term of opprobrium (Luz, *Matthew 8–20*, 449–50).

9. Matthew 18:17 says, "If the member refuses to listen to them," implying that the witnesses support the victim in his complaint.

10. Luz has a very extensive discussion of the various interpretations of Matthew 18:17, concluding that the hope that the individual might return is the more likely interpretation (Luz, *Matthew 8–20*, 450–53).

11. We are aware of the weak textual evidence for Luke 23:34. But attributing the saying to the early church means that the church understood and powerfully captured the meaning of Jesus' embodiment of forgiveness.

12. Desmond Tutu, *No Future without Forgiveness* (New York: Doubleday/Random House, 1999).

13. The story is told in numerous accounts. In this case, we found it at www.today .com/news/how-do-you-forgive-killer-mother-moves-past-tragedy-4B11203330.

14. See Roy F. Baumeister, Julie Juola Exline, and Kristin Sommer, "The Victim Role, Grudge Theory, and Two Dimensions of Forgiveness," in *Dimensions of Forgiveness: Psychological Research and Theological Perspectives*, ed. Everett L. Worthington Jr. (Philadelphia: Templeton Foundation Press, 1998).

15. See Baumeister et al., "Victim Role," 81, with more detailed discussion of grudge theory on 90–101.

16. That it is first of all the victim who must forgive is a main theme in Simon Wiesenthal, *The Sunflower: On the Possibilities and Limits of Forgiveness*, newly expanded ed. (New York: Schocken, 1998). While imprisoned during World War II, Wiesenthal was asked by a soldier who had committed an atrocity against Jews for forgiveness. He refused, because he felt he had no

right to forgive the soldier on behalf of others. The book explores whether he was right in doing that.

17. Chad M. Magnuson and Robert E. Enright, "The Church as Forgiving Community: An Initial Model," *Journal of Psychology and Theology* 36 (2008): 114–23.
18. Magnuson and Enright, "Church as Forgiving Community," 116.
19. Magnuson and Enright, "Church as Forgiving Community," 118.
20. The literature on forgiveness research is far too extensive to even begin to do it justice, but some examples may be mentioned, including the following: Everett L. Worthington Jr., ed., *Handbook of Forgiveness* (New York: Routledge, 2005); Michael E. McCullough, Kenneth I. Pargament, and Carl E. Thoresen, eds., *Forgiveness: Theory, Research, and Practice* (New York: Guilford, 2000); Robert D. Enright and Joanna North, eds., *Exploring Forgiveness* (Madison: University of Wisconsin Press, 1998); Everett L. Worthington Jr., ed., *Dimensions of Forgiveness: Psychological Research and Theological Perspectives* (West Conshohocken, PA: Templeton, 1998); and Dacher Keltner, Jason Marsh, and Jeremy Adam Smith, eds., *The Compassion Instinct: The Science of Human Goodness* (New York: Norton, 2010).

Chapter 10

1. Daniel Goleman, Richard Boyatzis, and Annie McKee, *Primal Leadership: Realizing the Power of Emotional Intelligence* (Cambridge, MA: Harvard Business School Press, 2002), 6–7; Goleman's emphasis. Goleman cites the studies to which he refers.
2. Walter Cannon, "'Voodoo' Death," *American Anthropologist* 44, no. 2 (1942): 182–90.
3. As a caveat, we witnessed some glaring exceptions to this in Alban Institute research. See Roy M. Oswald and Speed B. Leas, *The Inviting Church: A Study of New Member Assimilation* (Washington, DC: Alban Institute, 1987).
4. "Here we show that intranasal administration of oxytocin, a neuropeptide that plays a key role in social attachment and affiliation in non-human mammals, causes a substantial increase in trust among humans, thereby greatly increasing the benefits from social interactions." Michael Kosfeld, Markus Heinrichs, Paul J. Zak, Urs Fischbacher, and Ernst Fehr, "Oxytocin Increases Trust in Humans," *Nature* 135, no. 2 (June 2005).
5. Thomas Baumgartner, Markus Heinrichs, Aline Vonlanthen, Urs Fischbacher, and Ernst Fehr, "Oxytocin Shapes the Neural Circuitry of Trust and Trust Adaptation in Humans," *Neuron* 58, no. 4 (2008): 639–50.
6. Peter L. Steinke, *Healthy Congregations: A Systems Approach*, 2nd ed. (Herndon, VA: Alban Institute, 2006).

7. Roy M. Oswald and Robert E. Friedrich, *Discerning Your Congregation's Future: A Strategic and Spiritual Approach* (Washington, DC: Alban Institute, 1996).
8. M. Scott Peck, *The Different Drum: Community Making and Peace* (New York: Simon & Schuster, 1987).
9. Robert Putnam, *Bowling Alone: The Collapse and Revival of American Community* (New York: Simon & Schuster, 2000).

Chapter 11

1. Speed B. Leas, "Involuntary Termination of Clergy" (an Alban Institute research project).
2. Edwin Friedman, *Generation to Generation: Family Process in Church and Synagogue* (New York and London: Guilford Press, 1985; paperback edition, 2011), esp. 208–10. The notion of nonanxious leadership is discussed more broadly in Friedman's posthumously published book, *A Failure of Nerve: Leadership in the Age of the Quick Fix*, edited by Margaret M. Treadwell and Edward W. Beal (New York: Church Publishing, 2007).
3. Roy M. Oswald, *How to Build a Support Group for Your Ministry* (Eugene, OR: Wipf & Stock, 2005).
4. Ira Progoff, *At a Journal Workshop: Writing to Access the Power of the Unconscious and Evoke Creative Ability*, rev. ed. (New York: Tarcher/Putnam, 1992).
5. Center for EQ-HR Skills. See available Coaching Ministry, www.eqhrcenter. org or 301-432-8933.

Chapter 12

1. Howard Friend, "Failure to Form Basic Partnership: Resolving a Dilemma of New Pastorates," *Congregations*, a publication of the Alban Institute, January 2012.
2. For information on maintaining a long pastorate, see Roy M. Oswald, Gail D. Hinand, William Chris Hobgood, and Barton M. Lloyd, *New Visions for the Long Pastorate* (Herndon, VA: Alban Institute, 1983).
3. Melissa Korn, "B-Schools Know How You Think, But How Do You Feel?" *Wall Street Journal*, May 1, 2013.
4. Roy M. Oswald, *Finding Leaders for Tomorrow's Church: The Growing Crisis in Clergy Recruitment* (Herndon, VA: Alban Institute, 1993).
5. Roy M. Oswald, James Heath, and Ann Heath, *Beginning Ministry Together* (Herndon, VA: Alban Institute, 2003).

6. For more details, see Roy M. Oswald and Speed B. Leas, *The Inviting Church: A Study in New Member Assimilation* (Herndon, VA: Alban Institute, 1987).
7. For a good example of the spirituality of the "new monasticism," see Shane Claiborne, Jonathan Wilson-Hartgrove, and Enuma Okoro, *Common Prayer: Liturgy for Ordinary Radicals* (Grand Rapids, MI: Zondervan, 2010).
8. Studies are emerging that point out, for example, that wealth and power tend to diminish empathy. See Jennifer Stellar, Vida M. Manzo, Michael W. Kraus, and Dacher Keltner, "Class and Compassion: Socioeconomic Factors Predict Responses to Suffering," *Emotion* 12, no. 3 (June 2012): 449–59. In *The Psychopath Test: A Journey through the Madness Industry* (New York: Riverhead, 2012), Jon Ronson notes that the lack of empathy that is characteristic of psychopaths can be a valued asset in CEOs of large companies.

Appendix I

1. Daniel Goleman, *Emotional Intelligence*, 10th anniv. ed. (New York: Bantam, 2006). Also by Daniel Goleman: *The Meditative Mind*; *Vital Lies, Simple Truths*; *Working with Emotional Intelligence*; *Primal Leadership* (coauthor); *Destructive Emotions* (narrator); and *Social Intelligence*.
2. Richard J. Davidson, with Sharon Begley, *The Emotional Life of your Brain* (New York: Hudson Street, 2012).
3. MSCEIT (Mayer-Salovey-Caruso Emotional Intelligence Test), available to the general public from Multi-Health Systems, www.mhs.com. Supporting book, David Caruso and Peter Salovey, *The Emotionally Intelligent Manager* (San Francisco: Jossey-Bass, 2004).
4. Davidson and Begley, *The Emotional Life of Your Brain*, xv–xvii, 2–4.
5. Davidson and Begley, *The Emotional Life of Your Brain*, 43–65.
6. Davidson and Begley, *The Emotional Life of Your Brain*, 117–18, 121.

Appendix II

1. T. H. Holmes and R. H. Rahe are cited in Kenneth R. Pelletier, *Mind as Healer, Mind as Slayer* (New York: Dell, 1977), 108–14.

Lightning Source UK Ltd.
Milton Keynes UK
UKHW021135160919

349872UK00009B/2352/P